THE
Chocolate
Addict's
BAKING BOOK

Sabine Venier, creator of Also The Crumbs Please

PAGE STREET
PUBLISHING CO.

First published in 2020 by

Page Street Publishing Co.

27 Congress Street, Suite 105

Salem, MA 01970

www.pagestreetpublishing.com

Distributed by Macmillan, sales in Canada by The Canadian Manda Group.

24   23   22   21   2   3   4   5

ISBN-13: 978-1-64567-120-6

ISBN-10: 1-64567-120-8

Library of Congress Control Number: 2019957266

Cover and book design by Laura Benton for Page Street Publishing Co.

Photography by Sabine Venier

Printed and bound in the United States

THIS BOOK IS DEDICATED TO:

All of you wonderful people who love chocolate and baking and reading cookbooks. It's an honor to share my best and most loved chocolate recipes with you. I hope you will fill this cookbook with beautiful memories and love. Thank you so much from the bottom of my heart for letting me be a part of your life.

Also, to my husband, Mario, who supports me in everything I do. Thank you so much for trying everything in this cookbook and giving honest feedback and tips to create the most amazing chocolate cookbook of all time. Without you, this cookbook wouldn't exist at all. I love you.

CONTENTS

Introduction

As long as I can remember, our family tradition has been to bake together. It's usually my mother and me, but as soon as the holiday season is upon us, everyone in our family comes together and bakes. I think this is the reason I've developed such a strong and deep emotional connection to baking. It always makes me beyond happy to spend time together in the kitchen.

Baking has been a lifelong hobby for me, and for the last two years, it's also what I do for a living. Creating and baking recipes for my blog, Also The Crumbs Please, as well as brands and magazines, is such a fulfilling "job." It's hard to call it a job because it doesn't feel like a job at all. It's still very much my passion and my hobby. I'm more than grateful that this deep passion and also my dedication led to this cookbook.

When my cookbook publisher asked what I'd like to write about, it took me literally just one minute to come up with the idea of a chocolate cookbook. More than half of all the baking recipes I create contain chocolate. I'm a chocolate addict. No, screw that. I'm a chocolate freak! That describes it better. I can't imagine living one week without chocolate. Nope. Not going to happen. I need my weekly dose of chocolate, and lots of it.

I'm so excited to share all my favorite chocolate recipes with you! I know how cookbooks are treated in our home and the value they provide. I grew up with cookbooks, and it touches my heart to know that from now on this cookbook will be a part of your family and maybe handed down through generations. It's been an honor to put this book together for you, and I have done my utmost to provide you with my absolute best chocolate recipes that everyone in your family will love.

Some of these chocolate baking recipes have been family treasures for decades; some are newly developed for this book. But all of them have been tested and approved by my family, friends and me. I stand 100 percent behind each and every recipe in this book. You will find a collection of chocolate bars, brownies, breads, cakes, candy, cookies, cupcakes, muffins, pastries, pies, tarts and even no-bake baking recipes. Is that even a thing? No-bake baking? We'll make it a thing, okay?

It is very important to me that everyone who loves chocolate and baking will be satisfied with this cookbook. Before I even started to make a recipe list, I wrote down a list of different foods and flavors I absolutely wanted to include in this book, since I didn't want it to be just a collection of the most obvious and well-known chocolate baking recipes. Of course, this book contains classics, such as chocolate fudge cake and even chocolate chunk cookies, but you will also find very creative creations as well. You love chile? Avocado? Key lime? Honey? Bacon? Champagne? Rosemary? All of these and many, many more appear in this book. Whether you like milk, dark or white chocolate best, you'll find plenty of recipes that use your favorite. If you do not like one of the flavors in a recipe, you can always replace it, and you will find notes in each recipe to do so.

What is also important to me is that you get a real baking cookbook that is worth investing in and spending time with. So, be prepared to learn how to make chocolate croissants, chocolate pralines or chocolate brioche. Although there are many chocolate recipes in this book that are quick and easy to make, I'm proud to include these more advanced baking recipes as well, to help you expand your skills as a home baker.

All in all, you've purchased a chocolate baking book for every occasion and level of baking experience. I just love the idea that you can grow your baking skills with every chapter and learn to master more advanced recipes without any problems. Some recipes might not turn out looking exactly like my photos when you try them for the first time, but keep on baking and learn from your mistakes. Just for the record, my very first attempt to make macarons was a huge disaster, but I didn't give up, and as you can see, now I'm good enough to write a recipe teaching someone else how to make my favorite kind, Dark Chocolate Mint Macarons (page 52).

The most important thing is that you enjoy this cookbook and its recipes. No matter whether you're baking alone, with your family, your friends or you name it, this book is purely designed for fun. So, go ahead and get started!

Baking Tips

All recipes are written in detail to make sure you have success when you re-create them at home. However, here are a few more useful tips for your baking so you can be sure to bake exactly as I do.

PERCENTAGES OF COCOA IN CHOCOLATE

When I mention semisweet chocolate, I refer to chocolate that contains 50 to 60 percent cocoa. Why is this important to tell you? Well, the higher or the lower the percentages of the cocoa in the chocolate makes the recipe less or more sweet. So, when a recipe calls for semisweet chocolate, the amount of sugar in that recipe is balanced to work with that kind of chocolate. If I use any other chocolate with other percentages than this—70 percent, for example—I say so explicitly in the ingredients list.

CHOCOLATE BARS VS. CHOCOLATE CHIPS

I always specify what kind of chocolate I use for a recipe: bar-style or chips. Most of the time, I chop and melt high-quality chocolate bars for cake batters, frosting or ganache, rather than melting chocolate chips. The reason is that chocolate chips don't melt as smoothly and tenderly as bar-style chocolate normally does. You can use high-quality baking chocolate bars or even regular bars from a brand you love. I prefer to use chocolate bars made by Ghirardelli or Lindt.

DUTCH-PROCESSED VS. NATURAL COCOA POWDER

You will always read in the ingredients list which type of unsweetened cocoa powder I used for the recipe. The difference between Dutch-processed and natural is the acidity in the cocoa powder, which affects which leavening agent(s) you will use in the recipe. Whereas Dutch-processed cocoa powder needs baking powder to become active and help your baked goods rise, natural cocoa powder needs baking soda or a combination of baking soda and baking powder to do so. If you wish to substitute one kind of cocoa powder for the other, then you will need to make adjustments to the leavening agents in the recipe. Therefore, you need to know that baking soda is about three times as powerful as baking powder, or in a 1:3 ratio of baking soda to baking powder (e.g., ⅓ teaspoon of baking soda equals about 1 teaspoon of baking powder). Whenever an ingredients list contains neither baking powder nor baking soda, such as in brownie recipes, you can use whatever type of cocoa powder you prefer. In this case, I just listed the type of cocoa powder I used, so that you can re-create the flavor of the recipe as I made it, because these types of cocoa powder differ slightly in taste.

Whenever a recipe calls for room-temperature butter, that means that the butter should be slightly softened at room temperature for about 1 hour, but it must be still firm enough that when you press it with your fingers, you make just an indentation rather than gliding through the butter. It should be cool to the touch and soft, but also still firm enough that it is not greasy or runny.

ABOUT CREAM CHEESE

In recipes that call for cream cheese, you can use either brick-style or spreadable (but not whipped) cream cheese. Whichever you use, at the time you add it to the other ingredients, it must be soft. That means that you can use spreadable cream cheese right out of the fridge, but brick-style cream cheese should be at room temperature to be sufficiently soft.

A NOTE ON MEASURING INGREDIENTS

If you don't have a kitchen scale, please measure all dry ingredients, such as flour or cocoa powder, as follows: Use a regular tablespoon to spoon the dry ingredients into the measuring cup loosely, slowly and without packing it. Fill the cup until it is full and then carefully level it with the back of a knife, without pressing the ingredient into the cup, so as to avoid packing it. This is important because too much flour or cocoa powder, or any dry ingredient in general, creates a completely different texture and your baked goods very likely will end up dry, crumbly or dense.

As for measuring ingredients that need to be prepped: Whenever I list, for example, 1 cup (100 g) walnuts, chopped, I mean that you need to measure the walnuts whole and then chop them after measuring. On the other hand, 1 cup (120 g) chopped walnuts indicates that you need to chop walnuts first and then measure them (chopped will fill the cup more tightly than unchopped). Similarly, ½ cup (113 g [1 stick]) unsalted butter, melted, means that you measure the butter first and then melt it.

TEMPERATURE TALK

Always use an oven thermometer to ensure that your oven, once preheated, is at the correct temperature called for in the recipe. The temperature you set the oven to may not be accurate—it may be too hot or too cold, which could lead to different results, such as different textures or baking times. For example, if cookies don't spread, it could be that your oven is just too cold. On the other hand, if they spread too much, your oven could be too hot.

CROWD-PLEASING BARS AND BROWNIES

Isn't this a wonderful chapter to start this cookbook? Chocolate bars and brownies are so easy to make and suitable for every occasion. Think of The Best Chocolate Caramel Crunch Bars (page 12) for birthdays, or Boozy Kentucky Bourbon Walnut Chocolate Brownies (page 16) for potlucks, S'mores Chocolate Cheesecake Bars (page 15) for summer barbecues or loads of Rocky Road Scotcheroos Bars (page 20) for a cozy weekend with your family.

With these easy, minimal-cleanup recipes, the days that you even think about using a packaged brownie mix are officially over. You can literally make a couple of batches of these desserts within an hour and serve a whole crowd! Whether you're on the hunt for something crunchy or superfudgy, and no matter what kind of chocolate you crave, I've got you covered.

What more could chocolate lovers like you and me ask for?

If you are looking for the ultimate chocolate crunch bar experience, look no further! These supereasy bars come with a crispy, cookie-like base and they are topped with, yes, you guessed it, chocolate bars and crushed caramel candies. It's like eating cookies, milk chocolate bars and caramels all at the same time. Have you ever topped your chocolate bars with crushed caramel? If the answer is no, it's time to change that. Immediately. Just thinking about this delectable treat has me drooling.

Oh, and the best part? It's a one-bowl recipe. So, basically all you need is a bowl and an electric mixer.

The Best Chocolate Caramel Crunch Bars

YIELD: **15** BARS

1 cup (226 g [2 sticks]) unsalted butter, at room temperature

1 cup (200 g) packed light brown sugar

1 large egg yolk

2 tsp (10 ml) vanilla extract

2 cups (270 g) all-purpose flour, spooned and leveled

½ tsp salt

12 oz (340 g) bar-style milk chocolate (I used Hershey's Milk Chocolate Bars)

1 cup (100 g) walnuts, roughly chopped

½ cup (120 g) crushed hard caramel candies, such as Werther's

Preheat the oven to 350°F (175°C). Line a 9 x 13–inch (23 x 33–cm) baking pan with parchment paper with an overhang around the sides and set aside.

In a large bowl, using an electric mixer fitted with a paddle or whisk attachment, beat the butter, brown sugar, egg yolk and vanilla on medium speed until creamy and fluffy, 2 to 3 minutes. Add the flour and salt and mix to combine.

Transfer the dough to the prepared pan and press evenly into the bottom of the pan. Bake the bars for 25 to 30 minutes, or until golden brown.

Remove from the oven and place the chocolate bars, in a single layer, on top of the baked base; let sit for about 5 minutes, or until melted. Then, spread the melted chocolate evenly across the base and top with the walnuts and crushed caramels.

After 10 minutes, use the parchment to lift the bars out of the pan and let cool completely on a wire rack. Cut into 15 bars and store in an airtight container at room temperature for up to 4 days or freeze for up to 2 months.

If, like me, you love these very popular and yummy campfire treats, then you will go crazy over these s'mores bars. They come very close to the real deal. Imagine a crunchy graham cracker crust topped with creamy chocolate cheesecake filling and served with toasted marshmallows—these are s'mores 2.0.

S'mores Chocolate Cheesecake Bars

YIELD: 20 BITE-SIZE BARS

CRUST

2 cups (200 g) graham cracker crumbs, spooned and leveled

2 tbsp (25 g) sugar

5 tbsp (71 g) unsalted butter, melted

FILLING

1 lb (454 g) cream cheese, softened

½ cup (100 g) sugar

2 tbsp (11 g) unsweetened natural cocoa powder

1 tsp vanilla extract

1 large egg

3 oz (85 g) bar-style milk chocolate, melted

20 marshmallows

Preheat the oven to 350°F (175°C). Line a 9-inch (23-cm) square baking pan with parchment paper with an overhang around the sides and set aside.

Make the crust: In a medium bowl, using a wooden spoon or spatula, combine the graham cracker crumbs, sugar and butter until evenly moist. Then, transfer the crumbs to the prepared pan and press evenly into the bottom of the pan; this is best done with the base of a flat-bottomed cup. Bake the crust for 10 minutes.

While the crust bakes, make the filling: In a large bowl, using an electric mixer fitted with a paddle or whisk attachment, beat the cream cheese until creamy, about 2 minutes. Then, add the sugar, cocoa powder and vanilla and mix to combine, about 1 minute. Add the egg and whisk just to combine, 1 minute. Finally, add the melted chocolate and stir until smooth and well combined, about 1 minute. Transfer the filling to the prebaked crust and spread evenly. Bake for 28 to 32 minutes, or until the filling is set.

Remove from the oven and let cool completely in the pan. Then, use the parchment to lift the bars out of the pan and cut them into 20 pieces. Top with the marshmallows and toast them with a kitchen torch before serving. Store, without marshmallows on top, in an airtight container in the fridge for up to 2 days or freeze for up to 1 month.

NOTE: You can top the bars with meringue instead of marshmallows, if you prefer; see my favorite meringue recipe on page 134. In this case, add the meringue before cutting the baked bar into pieces. Do not freeze the meringue-topped bars.

The combination of superfudgy brownies with a crunchy, boozy bourbon and walnut topping is out of this world. Trust me, from one chocolate fan to another, even if you do not like bourbon or any kind of alcohol, you need to give this recipe a shot. Think of the bourbon as a uniquely flavorful extract. But if you'd still rather not add liquor to these brownies, then just leave it out without any replacement. But please, try it!

Boozy Kentucky Bourbon Walnut Chocolate Brownies

YIELD: **15** BROWNIES

TOPPING

2 cups (200 g) walnuts, chopped

¾ cup (150 g) packed dark brown sugar

¼ cup (60 ml) dark corn syrup

¼ cup (57 g [½ stick]) unsalted butter, melted

3 tbsp (45 ml) Kentucky bourbon

2 tsp (10 ml) vanilla extract

1 cup (170 g) semisweet chocolate chips

BROWNIES

¾ cup (170 g [1½ sticks]) unsalted butter, melted

¼ cup (60 ml) vegetable or canola oil

1½ cups (300 g) sugar

4 large eggs

1 cup (135 g) all-purpose flour, spooned and leveled

1 cup (85 g) unsweetened natural cocoa powder, spooned and leveled

1 tsp salt

Preheat the oven to 350°F (175°C). Line a baking sheet and also a 9 x 13-inch (23 x 33-cm) baking pan with parchment paper and set aside.

Make the topping: Place the walnuts, in a single layer, on the prepared baking sheet and toast them in the oven for 5 to 7 minutes, watching them closely to ensure that they don't burn. Then, remove from the oven and let cool for 15 minutes, or until cool enough to handle, then chop them.

Transfer the chopped walnuts, together with the brown sugar, corn syrup, melted butter, bourbon, vanilla and chocolate chips to a medium bowl and stir to combine. Set aside.

Make the brownies: In a large bowl, whisk together the melted butter, oil, sugar and eggs just until combined, about 1 minute. Then, sift in the flour, cocoa powder and salt and stir just to combine, another minute.

Transfer the brownie batter to the prepared baking pan and spoon the topping evenly on top. Bake for 22 to 28 minutes, or until the brownies don't jiggle anymore when the pan is moved and they are just set to touch. A toothpick inserted into the center should come out with a few crumbs attached to it. The time varies from oven to oven, so check the first time after 22 minutes and then frequently until they are done.

Remove from the oven and let cool in the pan for about 15 minutes—the brownies will continue to bake in the pan. Then, carefully lift the brownies out of the pan and transfer them to a wire rack to cool completely before cutting. Cut into 15 bars and store in an airtight container at room temperature for up to 4 days or freeze for up to 2 months.

These are one of my absolute favorite treats. Imagine heaven made out of chocolate—that's how I can describe these bars. Seriously. The words double chocolate don't promise too much. As a chocolate addict, you will sink peacefully into your chair with a big, fat smile on your face after the very first bite. You can't do much wrong with this recipe; just be careful not to overmix or overbake these bars, or they could turn out cakey instead of chewy.

Ultrachewy Double Chocolate Oatmeal Bars

YIELD: **15** BARS

1 cup (226 g [2 sticks]) unsalted butter, at room temperature

1 cup (200 g) packed light brown sugar

½ cup (100 g) sugar

2 large eggs

2 tsp (10 ml) vanilla extract

1¼ cups (169 g) all-purpose flour, spooned and leveled

¼ cup (21 g) unsweetened natural cocoa powder, spooned and leveled

1 tsp baking soda

1 tsp salt

2 cups (200 g) old-fashioned rolled oats

1½ cups (255 g) semisweet chocolate chips

Preheat the oven to 350°F (175°C). Line a 9 x 13-inch (23 x 33–cm) baking pan with parchment paper with an overhang around the sides and set aside.

In a large bowl, using an electric mixer fitted with a paddle or whisk attachment, beat the butter and both sugars on medium speed until creamy, about 2 minutes. Then, add the eggs and vanilla and stir until well combined, 1 to 2 minutes. Add the flour, cocoa powder, baking soda and salt and mix to combine, about 1 minute. Stir in the oats and the chocolate chips just to combine.

Transfer to the prepared pan and spread evenly. Bake for 18 to 20 minutes. A toothpick inserted into in the center should come out clean.

Remove from the oven and let cool in the pan for about 15 minutes. Then, use the parchment to lift the bars out of the pan and transfer to a wire rack to let cool completely. Cut into 15 bars and store in an airtight container at room temperature for up to 4 days or freeze for up to 2 months.

This recipe wakes up my inner kid! I'm thrilled to share my marriage of two beloved childhood sweet treats: rocky road candies and scotcheroos. These bars are everything that kids and grown-up kids could ask for: a crunchy peanut buttery and chocolaty base topped with superdelicious milk chocolate, colorful mini marshmallows and peanuts. Instead of regular crispy rice cereal, I used chocolate-flavored for an even more intense chocolate taste. Let's be kids again and have some fun trying these sweets!

Rocky Road Scotcheroos Bars

YIELD: **20** BARS

BARS

6 cups (300 g) chocolate crispy rice cereal, such as Rice Krispies

1 cup (240 ml) light corn syrup

1 cup (200 g) sugar

1 tbsp (14 g) unsalted butter

1 cup (250 g) creamy peanut butter

1 tsp vanilla extract

1 tsp butterscotch extract

Pinch of salt

TOPPING

3 cups (75 g) mini marshmallows

¼ cup (38 g) peanuts, chopped

12 oz (340 g) bar-style milk chocolate, chopped

¼ cup (42 g) butterscotch chips

Line a 9 x 13–inch (23 x 33–cm) baking pan with parchment paper with an overhang around the sides and set aside.

Make the bars: Place the cereal in a large bowl and set aside.

In a heavy-bottomed saucepan over medium heat, combine the corn syrup, sugar and butter and stir until the sugar is completely dissolved, 3 to 5 minutes. Do not bring to a boil. Remove from the heat, stir in the peanut butter, vanilla and butterscotch extract and add salt to taste. Stir until well combined, 30 to 60 seconds. Pour the mixture over the cereal and stir until well incorporated.

Transfer the mixture to the prepared pan, press evenly into the bottom of the pan and set aside.

Make the topping: In a large bowl, combine the mini marshmallows and peanuts, then set aside.

In a microwave-safe bowl, combine the chocolate and butterscotch chips and microwave on a medium setting, stirring every 20 seconds until melted, about 2 minutes. Pour the chocolate over the marshmallow mixture and stir until everything is evenly coated with chocolate. Then, spoon the mixture on top of the cereal mixture and distribute evenly.

Let cool and harden completely before you cut into 20 bars. Store in an airtight container at room temperature for up to 5 days.

NOTE: If you can't find butterscotch chips for the topping, replace them 1:1 with peanut butter chips and add ½ teaspoon of butterscotch extract before you melt the chips in the microwave.

Get yourself ready for this ridiculously delicious chocolate treat. This recipe combines a couple of my favorite flavors—cherries, cream cheese and, of course, chocolate! I mean, what's not to love here? I think that this is the ultimate dessert to celebrate cherry season and beyond. Always try to go for fresh cherries if possible, but don't worry if they're not in season. You can use either fresh or frozen cherries for these brownies. Even pickled cherries work! Just make sure to thaw frozen cherries or drain pickled cherries before you add them.

Cherry Cheesecake Swirl Chocolate Brownies

YIELD: 15 BARS

BROWNIES

6 oz (170 g) bar-style semisweet chocolate, finely chopped

1 cup (226 g [2 sticks]) unsalted butter, at room temperature

4 large eggs

¾ cup (150 g) packed light brown sugar

¾ cup (150 g) sugar

2 tsp (10 ml) vanilla extract

1½ cups (203 g) all-purpose flour, spooned and leveled

½ cup (43 g) unsweetened Dutch-processed cocoa powder, spooned and leveled

1 tsp salt

2 cups (250 g) pitted and halved fresh cherries

CHEESECAKE SWIRL

8 oz (227 g) cream cheese, softened

¼ cup (50 g) sugar

1 large egg yolk

½ cup (170 g) cherry preserves or jam

Preheat the oven to 350°F (175°C). Line a 9 x 13–inch (23 x 33–cm) baking pan with parchment paper with an overhang around the sides and set aside.

Make the brownies: In a microwave-safe bowl, combine the chocolate and butter and microwave on a medium setting for about 2 minutes, or until completely melted and mixed, stirring every 20 seconds. Then, set aside.

In a large bowl, whisk together the eggs, both sugars and vanilla, just to combine, about 1 minute. Stir in the chocolate mixture just to incorporate, about 30 seconds. Sift in the flour, cocoa powder and salt and stir to combine, about 1 minute. Fold in the cherries and set aside.

Make the cheesecake swirl: In a medium bowl, stir together the cream cheese, sugar, egg yolk and cherry preserves until well mixed, smooth and no lumps remain, 1 to 2 minutes.

Spoon about half of the brownie batter into the prepared pan and spread evenly. Then, alternately spoon dollops of the cheesecake swirl and the remaining brownie batter on top of the brownie batter in the pan. When you're done, run a knife through the pan to draw a swirl.

Bake for 27 to 35 minutes, or until the brownies don't jiggle anymore when the pan is slightly moved and they are just set to the touch. A toothpick inserted into the center should come out with a few crumbs attached to it. The time varies from oven to oven, so check the first time after 27 minutes and then check frequently, every 2 minutes, until they are done.

Remove from the oven and let cool in the pan for about 20 minutes; the brownies will continue to bake in the pan. Then, transfer carefully to a wire rack and let cool completely before cutting. Cut into 15 bars and store in an airtight container in the fridge for up to 2 days or freeze for up to 2 months. Let come to room temperature before serving.

If you're craving an adult kind of chocolate treat, this recipe is the choice for you! I think that chocolate and coffee are such a wonderful combination, so delicious together. I decided to use Kahlúa, which is a coffee liqueur, because it made so much sense to pair it with the espresso in the brownies. If you do not want to add alcohol to your brownie bites, just replace the Kahlúa with strong brewed coffee, or if you want to make them kid-friendly, use milk.

Espresso Kahlúa Chocolate Brownie Bites

YIELD: **20** BROWNIE BITES

Nonstick spray, for pans

1 cup (226 g [2 sticks]) unsalted butter, melted

1 cup (200 g) packed dark brown sugar

½ cup (100 g) sugar

4 large eggs

½ cup (120 ml) Kahlúa

2 tsp (10 ml) vanilla extract

1½ cups (203 g) all-purpose flour, spooned and leveled

1 cup (85 g) unsweetened natural cocoa powder, spooned and leveled

2 tsp (4 g) espresso powder

1 tsp salt

Preheat the oven to 350°F (175°C). Spray two 12-well muffin pans with nonstick spray and set aside.

In a large bowl, whisk together the melted butter, sugars, eggs, Kahlúa and vanilla just until combined, about 1 minute. Then, sift in the flour, cocoa powder, espresso powder and salt and stir just to combine, another minute.

Spoon the batter into the prepared muffin wells until about three-quarters full. Bake for 15 to 17 minutes, or until the brownie bites bounce back to the touch. Do not overbake, or else the brownie bites will end up dry rather than moist and fudgy.

Remove from the oven and let cool in the pans for about 5 minutes. Then, transfer to a wire rack and let cool before serving. Store in an airtight container at room temperature for up to 3 days or freeze for up to 2 months.

These bars always make me think about Halloween. Why? Because they are scary . . . scary delicious! Ha, that was a good one, right? Let's be serious. We all know and agree that pumpkin and chocolate is an awesome combination. Enjoy these supermoist, dense and perfectly spiced bars all year round by using canned pumpkin puree when pumpkin is not in season. Call me crazy, but I would totally eat them on a 100°F (38°C) summer day with a huge scoop of vanilla ice cream.

Pumpkin Chocolate Chip Bars

YIELD: 15 BARS

1 cup (226 g [2 sticks]) unsalted butter, at room temperature

1 cup (200 g) packed light brown sugar

1 large egg

1 tsp vanilla extract

1 cup (226 g) pumpkin puree (not pumpkin pie filling!)

2 cups (270 g) all-purpose flour, spooned and leveled

1 tsp baking powder

1 tsp ground cinnamon

½ tsp ground ginger

¼ tsp ground nutmeg

¼ tsp ground allspice

⅛ tsp ground cloves

2 cups (340 g) semisweet chocolate chips

Preheat the oven to 350°F (175°C). Line a 9 x 13–inch (23 x 33–cm) baking pan with parchment paper with an overhang around the sides and set aside.

In a large bowl, using an electric mixer fitted with a paddle or whisk attachment, cream the butter and brown sugar on medium speed until creamy and fluffy, about 2 minutes. Then, add the egg and vanilla and stir until well combined, about 1 minute. Add the pumpkin puree and mix to combine, then set aside.

In a medium bowl, stir together the flour, baking powder, cinnamon, ginger, nutmeg, allspice and cloves. Add the flour mixture to the butter mixture and stir until well combined, 1 to 2 minutes. Stir in the chocolate chips just to incorporate.

Transfer the batter to the prepared pan and spread evenly. Bake for 22 to 25 minutes, or until a toothpick inserted into the center comes out clean.

Remove from the oven and let cool in the pan for about 15 minutes. Then, use the parchment to lift the bars out of the pan and transfer to a wire rack to cool completely. Cut into 15 bars and store in an airtight container at room temperature for up to 3 days or freeze for up to 2 months.

I'm happy to share this wonderful creation with you because olive oil in chocolate bars is ultradelicious. The olive oil supports the taste of these bars in such a great way! This recipe is definitely a crowd-pleaser and the perfect treat for your next party. They'll be sure to impress friends and family.

Zucchini Chocolate Olive Oil Bars

YIELD: 15 BARS

4 large eggs

1 cup (240 ml) high-quality olive oil

1 cup (200 g) sugar

1 cup (200 g) packed light brown sugar

2 tsp (10 ml) vanilla extract

2 cups (270 g) all-purpose flour, spooned and leveled

1 cup (85 g) unsweetened Dutch-processed cocoa, spooned and leveled

2 tsp (8 g) baking powder

1 tsp salt

1½ cups (255 g) semisweet chocolate chips

3 cups (450 g) squeezed shredded zucchini (2 to 3 medium zucchini)

Preheat the oven to 350°F (175°C). Line a 9 x 13–inch (23 x 33–cm) baking pan with parchment paper with an overhang around the sides and set aside.

In a large bowl, whisk together the eggs, olive oil, both sugars and vanilla just to combine, about 1 minute. Sift in the flour, cocoa powder, baking powder and salt and whisk to combine, 1 minute. Then, fold in the chocolate chips and zucchini until well incorporated.

Transfer the batter to the prepared pan and spread evenly. Bake for 27 to 32 minutes, or until a toothpick inserted into the center comes out clean.

Remove from the oven and let cool in the pan completely. Then, use the parchment to lift out of the pan and cut into 15 bars. Store in an airtight container at room temperature for up to 2 days or freeze for up to 1 month.

NOTES: I highly recommend using high-quality olive oil because the taste and quality of the oil have a big impact on the bars.

Make sure that you squeeze the water out of the shredded zucchini before measuring and adding it. One strong squeeze is enough, though.

These blondies are a fantastic way to satisfy your love for white chocolate. Did you know that carrots and white chocolate are a fantastic match? It's just epic to combine these fudgy blondies with a white chocolate cream cheese swirl. Did I mention that there are also white chocolate chunks in the bars themselves? This recipe is a white chocolate lovers' dream.

White Chocolate Carrot Cake Blondies

YIELD: **15** BARS

BLONDIES

¾ cup (170 g [1½ sticks]) unsalted butter, melted

¾ cup (150 g) packed light brown sugar

¾ cup (150 g) sugar

2 large eggs

1 tsp vanilla extract

2 cups (270 g) all-purpose flour, spooned and leveled

1 tsp salt

2 cups (300 g) shredded carrot

1½ cups (255 g) white chocolate chunks or chips

CREAM CHEESE SWIRL

8 oz (227 g) cream cheese, softened

1 large egg yolk

¼ cup (50 g) sugar

1 tsp vanilla extract

6 oz (170 g) bar-style white chocolate, melted

Preheat the oven to 350°F (175°C). Line a 9 x 13-inch (23 x 33-cm) baking pan with parchment paper with an overhang around the sides and set aside.

Make the blondie batter: In a large bowl, whisk together the melted butter, both sugars, eggs and vanilla just to combine, about 1 minute. Sift in the flour and salt and whisk to combine, about 1 minute. Then, fold in the shredded carrot and chocolate chunks just to incorporate and set aside.

Make the cream cheese swirl: In a medium bowl, using an electric mixer fitted with a whisk or paddle attachment, mix the cream cheese on medium speed until smooth, 1 to 2 minutes. Then, add the egg yolk, sugar and vanilla and mix just to combine, 1 minute. Stir in the melted chocolate just until incorporated.

Alternately spoon dollops of blondie batter and cream cheese swirl into the prepared pan and bake for 25 to 30 minutes, or until the edges are lightly browned and the center is just set.

Remove from the oven and let cool in the pan completely. Then, use the parchment to lift the bars out of the pan. Cut into 15 bars. Store in an airtight container in the fridge for up to 2 days or freeze for up to 1 month. Let the bars come to room temperature before serving.

NOTE: Either white chocolate bars chopped into chunks or white chocolate chips work for the blondie batter. However, for the cream cheese filling, melt only high-quality chocolate bars because melted chocolate chips make the swirl crumbly and dry.

IRRESISTIBLE COOKIES

What kind of chocolate dessert book would this be without a chapter dedicated to cookies? I'm thrilled to introduce you to my most loved chocolate cookie recipes of all time. It was very challenging to limit this chapter to just a few recipes because, come on, chocolate cookies? I could easily write a whole chocolate cookie cookbook!

Expect everything from Dark Chocolate Mint Macarons (page 52), to chewy Thick Cranberry Oatmeal White Chocolate Chip Cookies (page 51), to Baked Chocolate Churro Cookie Sandwiches (page 44), to a giant Guinness Pretzel Chocolate Skillet Cookie (page 43), to Superchewy Chocolate Snickerdoodles (page 36). Also, you will find Caramel-Stuffed Chocolate Cookies with Sea Salt (page 35), Ultrathin Chocolate Cashew Cookies (page 39), among others, within this chapter.

I personally love chocolate cookies so much because of how easy they are to make! With this chapter, you'll add new varieties of them to your baking repertoire.

These chewy chocolate cookies, with a gooey caramel center and topped with flaky sea salt, are what my dreams are made of. Among all the great chocolate cookies in this book, this is one of my top favorites and a frequent guest on weekends when Mario and I are alone and binge-watching something on Netflix. It's kind of ridiculous to share storage tips for these cookies because they won't survive any longer than a day, at least not in our home.

Caramel-Stuffed Chocolate Cookies with Sea Salt

YIELD: **12** COOKIES

1 cup (135 g) all-purpose flour, spooned and leveled

½ cup (43 g) unsweetened natural cocoa powder, spooned and leveled

½ tsp baking soda

¼ tsp salt

½ cup (113 g [1 stick]) unsalted butter, at room temperature

¼ cup (50 g) packed light brown sugar

¾ cup (150 g) sugar

1 large egg

2 tsp (10 ml) vanilla extract

12 soft caramel candies, such as Kraft or Werther's

1 tsp flaky sea salt

Preheat the oven to 350°F (175°C). Line two baking sheets with parchment paper and set aside.

In a medium bowl, stir together the flour, cocoa powder, baking soda and salt and set aside.

In a large bowl, using an electric mixer fitted with a paddle or whisk attachment, mix the butter and both sugars on medium speed just until combined, about 1 minute. Then, add the egg and vanilla and mix for about 30 seconds, just until combined. Add the flour mixture and mix until incorporated, about 1 minute.

Scoop 12 equal-sized balls (about 2 to 3 tablespoons [45 to 50 g] each) of cookie dough. Divide each ball in half, place a piece of caramel on the middle of one dough half and then roll the dough halves back into a ball until no caramel is visible anymore. Arrange 6 completed balls, spaced about 3 inches (7.5 cm) apart, on each baking sheet and lightly sprinkle with the sea salt. Bake one sheet at a time for 10 to 12 minutes, or until dry on top.

Remove from the oven and let cool for about 5 minutes, or until firm enough to move. Then, transfer to a wire rack and let cool completely. The cookies will stay fresh in an airtight container at room temperature for up to 4 days or freeze for up to 2 months.

NOTE: You can use this cookie dough recipe as a basic chewy chocolate cookie recipe and fill it with any mix-ins you like, such as peanut butter chips, toffee bits, chopped macadamias or white chocolate chips, just to name a few.

Expect a chocolate overload with these finger-licking snickerdoodles. Their texture is so soft and buttery that I would love to lie in it and eat my way through. I haven't baked regular snickerdoodles for years, ever since I discovered this recipe. It calls for cocoa powder and cinnamon in both the cookie dough and the coating so actually, there is double chocolate and double cinnamon. Sounds awesome, right? It truly is.

Superchewy Chocolate Snickerdoodles

YIELD: 12 COOKIES

COATING

3 tbsp (38 g) sugar

1 tsp ground cinnamon

½ tsp unsweetened natural cocoa powder

COOKIES

½ cup (113 g [1 stick]) unsalted butter, at room temperature

¾ cup (150 g) sugar

¼ cup (50 g) packed light brown sugar

1 large egg

1 tsp vanilla extract

1 cup (135 g) all-purpose flour, spooned and leveled

½ cup (43 g) unsweetened natural cocoa powder, spooned and leveled

½ tsp baking soda

½ tsp ground cinnamon

¼ tsp salt

Preheat the oven to 375°F (190°C). Line two baking sheets with parchment paper and set aside.

Make the coating: In a small bowl, whisk together the granulated sugar, cinnamon and cocoa powder and set aside.

Make the cookie dough: In a large bowl, using an electric mixer fitted with a paddle or whisk attachment, mix the butter and both sugars on medium speed just until combined, about 1 minute. Then, add the egg and vanilla and mix for about 30 seconds, or just until combined. Add the flour, cocoa powder, baking soda, cinnamon and salt and mix until incorporated, about 1 minute.

Scoop 12 equal-sized balls (about 2 to 3 tablespoons [45 to 50 g] each) of cookie dough and roll in the coating mixture to cover them entirely. Place 6 cookies, about 3 inches (7.5 cm) apart, on each prepared baking sheet. Bake one sheet at a time for 8 to 9 minutes, or until the cookies look puffy and dry.

Remove from the oven and let cool on the baking sheet for about 5 minutes, or until firm enough to move. Then, transfer to a wire rack and let cool completely. The cookies will stay fresh in an airtight container at room temperature for up to 4 days or freeze for up to 2 months.

NOTE: Make sure that you mix the cookie dough as little as possible, to achieve superchewy chocolate snickerdoodles. Overmixing is a common reason that cookies end up unintentionally cakey instead.

Do you see these cookies? I mean, can a chocolate cookie get any thinner than this? I doubt it. Although the majority of the cookies I eat are thicker and chewy, I love to make these superthin cookies as well. They are perfect for dunking into a mug of milk or hot chocolate. The cashews are the ideal nuts for these cookies, although you could use any other nuts that you like. And because they are so thin, it's okay to eat more of them—am I right?

Ultrathin Chocolate Cashew Cookies

YIELD: **12** COOKIES

1 cup (135 g) all-purpose flour, spooned and leveled

⅓ cup (28 g) unsweetened natural cocoa powder, spooned and leveled

½ tsp baking soda

¼ tsp salt

½ cup (113 g [1 stick]) unsalted butter, melted

½ cup (100 g) sugar

⅓ cup (67 g) packed light brown sugar

1 large egg

1 tsp vanilla extract

2 tbsp (30 ml) corn syrup

1 tbsp (15 ml) milk

1 cup (130 g) roasted cashews, chopped

Preheat the oven to 375°F (190°C). Line two or three baking sheets with parchment paper and set aside.

In a medium bowl, stir together the flour, cocoa, baking soda and salt and set aside.

In a large bowl, using an electric mixer fitted with a paddle or whisk attachment, mix the melted butter and both sugars on medium speed just until combined, about 1 minute. Then, add the egg, vanilla, corn syrup and milk and mix for about 30 seconds, just until combined. Add the flour mixture and mix until incorporated, about 1 minute. Then, stir in the cashews to incorporate.

Scoop 12 equal-sized balls (about 2 to 3 tablespoons [55 to 60 g]) of cookie dough and place 4 cookies, spaced 3 to 4 inches (7.5 to 10 cm) apart, on each prepared baking sheet. Bake one sheet at a time for 12 to 13 minutes, or until the cookies look crinkled, flat and dry.

Remove from the oven and let cool for about 5 minutes on the baking sheet, or until firm enough to move. Then, transfer to a wire rack and let cool completely. The cookies will stay fresh in an airtight container at room temperature for up to 4 days or freeze for up to 2 months.

NOTE: If you can't find or don't want to use corn syrup, you can go for golden syrup, honey or pure maple syrup instead. If you decide to leave it out completely, the cookies won't be as flat as in the photo.

I clearly remember baking these cookies for the first time, about a decade ago. After I was done baking and assembling them, I put them away and went out to the store. When I came home, Mario was already there with a friend of his. They thanked me for the cookies, which they said were so delicious that they were gone within ten minutes. So, they ate all the cookies, before I had a chance to try one! At the time, I was a bit upset that they hadn't left even one for me. This was so unusual for Mario, but looking back, I totally understand. After eating one, you cannot stop eating these cookies until somebody takes them away from you or they are gone. So, I don't blame them . . . anymore.

Coconut Chocolate Shortbread Cookies

YIELD: **24** COOKIES

½ cup (113 g [1 stick]) unsalted butter, at room temperature

¼ cup (50 g) sugar

1 cup (135 g) all-purpose flour, spooned and leveled

¼ cup (21 g) unsweetened natural cocoa powder, spooned and leveled

⅛ tsp salt

1½ cups (150 g) unsweetened shredded coconut flakes

7.5 oz (212 g) soft caramel candy, such as Kraft or Werther's

1 tbsp (15 ml) milk

3 oz (85 g) bar-style semisweet chocolate, melted

In a large bowl, using an electric mixer fitted with a whisk attachment, cream the butter and sugar on medium speed until soft and fluffy, 2 to 3 minutes. Then, add the flour, cocoa powder and salt and mix until the dough comes together, 1 to 2 minutes. Transfer to a sheet of plastic wrap. Roll into a log about 1 inch (2.5 cm) in diameter and wrap tightly. Refrigerate for at least 4 hours.

Preheat the oven to 350°F (175°C). Line two baking sheets with parchment paper and set aside.

Cut the dough log into ¼-inch (6-mm)-thick slices and place about 1 inch (2.5 cm) apart on the prepared baking sheets. Bake one sheet at a time for 10 to 11 minutes, or until the cookies look puffy and dry. Remove from the oven and let cool on the baking sheet for about 5 minutes, or until firm enough to move. Then, transfer to a wire rack and let cool for about 15 minutes.

While the cookies cool, spread the coconut flakes on an ungreased baking sheet and toast them at 300°F (150°C) for 5 to 8 minutes, watching them closely because they can burn very quickly. Remove from the oven and let cool while you prepare the caramel.

Place the caramels and milk in a microwave-safe bowl and microwave on a medium setting, stirring every 20 seconds, for about 2 minutes, or until the caramels are completely melted and combined with the milk.

Spread about ½ teaspoon of the caramel mixture on top of each cookie. Then, in a medium bowl, quickly combine the rest of the caramel mixture with the toasted coconut. Press about 1 tablespoon (15 g) of the coconut mixture on top of each cookie.

Drizzle the melted chocolate on top of the cookies or dunk their bottoms into the chocolate, according to your preference. The cookies will stay fresh in an airtight container at room temperature for up to 4 days or freeze for up to 1 month.

What is better than a dozen or two small chocolate cookies? One big chocolate cookie, of course. When you have friends over for Friday night dinner, this is an appropriate way to end the meal. Take the chocolate skillet cookie out of the oven, let it cool a bit, then top it with loads of chocolate ice cream. Next, grab a spoon and go for it! The cooked Guinness syrup in this skillet cookie adds an incredibly deep flavor and the pretzels add a bit of a crunch to it. It's a pleasure to eat this big skillet cookie with family and friends.

Guinness Pretzel Chocolate Skillet Cookie

YIELD: **12** SERVINGS

GUINNESS SYRUP

1 (11.2-oz [330-ml]) bottle Guinness stout

¼ cup (50 g) packed dark brown sugar

SKILLET COOKIE

1½ cups (203 g) all-purpose flour, spooned and leveled

½ cup (43 g) unsweetened natural cocoa powder, spooned and leveled

¾ tsp baking soda

½ tsp salt

¾ cup (150 g [1½ sticks]) unsalted butter

1 cup (200 g) packed dark brown sugar

½ cup (100 g) sugar

2 large eggs

2 tsp (10 ml) vanilla extract

1 cup (170 g) semisweet chocolate chips

2 cups (100 g) crushed pretzels

SERVING SUGGESTIONS

Ice cream and chocolate syrup

Make the Guinness syrup: In a medium saucepan over medium heat, bring the Guinness and brown sugar to a boil. Stirring occasionally, cook for 15 to 20 minutes or until it gets thick and is reduced to ⅓ cup (80 ml). Then, set aside.

Preheat the oven to 350°F (175°C).

Make the skillet cookie: In a medium bowl, stir together the flour, cocoa powder, baking soda and salt and set aside.

In a 10-inch (25-cm) cast-iron skillet over medium heat, melt the butter. Add both sugars and the cooked Guinness syrup and stir to combine. Remove from the heat and let cool for 5 minutes.

Add the eggs and vanilla and stir to combine. Fold in the flour mixture just until incorporated. Then, fold in the chocolate chips and pretzels until well combined. Transfer the skillet to the oven and bake for 25 to 30 minutes, or until the top looks set and dry.

Remove from the oven and let the cookie cool in the skillet for 20 to 30 minutes before serving. Garnish with ice cream and chocolate syrup, if desired. Store, covered, at room temperature for up to 1 day.

NOTE: If you want to try this chocolate skillet cookie without Guinness, you simply can leave out the syrup and don't need any substitution for it.

Buttery, tenderly-melting cookies covered in cinnamon sugar and filled with chocolate cream cheese frosting, these sandwich treats have it all. I have to warn you: Don't lick the chocolate frosting from a spoon before you fill the cookies. You won't have enough left for the cookies, because you will catch yourself spooning up half of the bowl in no time!

Baked Chocolate Churro Cookie Sandwiches

YIELD: **12** TO **14** SANDWICH COOKIES

COATING

½ cup (100 g) sugar

1½ tsp (4 g) ground cinnamon

COOKIES

1 cup (226 g [2 sticks]) unsalted butter, at room temperature

1 cup (120 g) unpacked powdered sugar, sifted

4 large egg yolks

2 tbsp (30 ml) milk

1 tsp vanilla extract

⅛ tsp salt

2½ cups (338 g) all-purpose flour, spooned and leveled

FILLING

½ cup (113 g [1 stick]) unsalted butter, at room temperature

2 oz (56 g) cream cheese, softened

¼ cup (74 g) chocolate spread, such as Nutella

1 tsp vanilla extract

1 cup (120 g) unpacked powdered sugar, sifted

¼ cup (21 g) unsweetened natural cocoa powder, spooned and leveled

Pinch of salt

Preheat the oven to 350°F (175°C).

Make the coating: In a small bowl, combine the sugar and cinnamon and set aside.

Make the cookies: In a large bowl, using an electric mixer fitted with a paddle or whisk attachment, mix the butter on medium speed until creamy, about 2 minutes. Add the powdered sugar and mix to incorporate, about 1 minute. Then, stir in the egg yolks, milk, vanilla and salt and continue to mix for another 1 to 2 minutes, or until everything is incorporated. Slowly mix in the flour just to combine, 1 to 2 minutes.

Spoon one-quarter of the batter into a piping bag fitted with an open star piping tip (I use Wilton 8B). First, pipe a little dot in each corner of one or two baking sheets and place a sheet of parchment paper on top. This helps the paper stick to the pan so it doesn't move around while you pipe the cookies. Then, pipe a 2-inch (5-cm) spiral of batter onto the prepared baking sheet, starting in the middle and moving the tip outward in a circular fashion. Please make sure that there are no gaps within your spiral. Pipe more spirals about 2 inches (5 cm) apart. Repeat with another quarter of cookie dough and pipe additional spirals onto the prepared baking sheets, until you run out of dough.

Bake one baking sheet at a time for 9 to 10 minutes, or until the cookies look dry and pale. Remove from the oven and let cool on the baking sheet for 5 to 10 minutes, or until firm enough to move. Then, roll the cookies in the coating and transfer to a wire rack to cool completely.

Make the filling: In a large bowl, with an electric mixer fitted with a whisk or paddle attachment, beat the butter on medium-high speed until very soft and fluffy, 2 to 3 minutes. Add the cream cheese and mix until smooth and combined, 1 to 2 minutes. Then, add the chocolate spread and vanilla and mix to incorporate, another minute. Stir in the powdered sugar and cocoa powder and whisk until creamy and smooth, 1 to 2 minutes. Add a pinch of salt, or to taste.

Pipe or spread the chocolate filling on the bottom of one cookie and top with another cookie to create a sandwich (each bottom against the other). Repeat until you run out of filling and cookies. Store in an airtight container at room temperature for up to 2 days or freeze for up to 1 month.

Peanut butter and chocolate are meant for each other and have a special place in my heart. So, it was quite apparent that there needed to be a chocolate and peanut butter cookie recipe in this book. And we all love peanut butter cookies anyway, don't we? Let's make them even better by adding cocoa powder.

Soft Chocolate Peanut Butter Cookies

YIELD: 18 COOKIES

1 cup (135 g) all-purpose flour, spooned and leveled

¼ cup (21 g) unsweetened natural cocoa powder, spooned and leveled

½ tsp baking powder

½ tsp baking soda

¼ tsp salt

½ cup (113 g [1 stick]) unsalted butter, at room temperature

½ cup (100 g) sugar

½ cup (100 g) packed light brown sugar

1 cup (250 g) creamy peanut butter

1 large egg

1 tsp vanilla extract

Preheat the oven to 350°F (175°C). Line two baking sheets with parchment paper and set aside.

In a medium bowl, stir together the flour, cocoa powder, baking powder, baking soda and salt and set aside.

In a large bowl, using an electric mixer fitted with a paddle or whisk attachment, mix the butter and both sugars on medium speed just until combined, about 1 minute. Then, add the peanut butter, egg and vanilla and mix for about 30 seconds, or just until combined. Add the flour mixture and mix until incorporated, about 1 minute.

Scoop 18 equal-sized balls (about 2 to 3 tablespoons [45 to 50 g] each) of cookie dough and place 9 cookies, spaced about 2 inches (5 cm) apart, on each prepared baking sheet. Then, press the tines of a fork on top of each cookie to create a crisscross pattern. Bake one sheet at a time for 9 to 10 minutes, or until the cookies look puffy and dry.

Remove from the oven and let cool on the baking sheet for about 5 minutes, or until firm enough to move. Then, transfer to a wire rack and let cool completely. The cookies will stay fresh in an airtight container at room temperature for up to 4 days or freeze for up to 2 months.

NOTE: You can dunk one side of the cookies into ½ cup (120 ml) of melted chocolate and sprinkle with ¼ cup (38 g) of chopped peanuts, if desired.

This is my go-to classic chocolate chip cookie recipe. I just enhanced it by adding chopped milk chocolate bars instead of regular chocolate chips. Chocolate chips are delicious, no doubt, but sometimes I prefer chopped chocolate chunks in my cookies. It takes them to the next level! These cookies are soft and chewy with crispy edges—basically, how a perfect cookie should be. The addition of tenderly-melting chocolate bars is just yum.

Milk Chocolate Chunk Cookies

YIELD: **12** COOKIES

½ cup (113 g [1 stick]) unsalted butter, at room temperature

½ cup (100 g) sugar

¼ cup (50 g) packed light brown sugar

1 large egg

1 tsp vanilla extract

1½ cups (203 g) all-purpose flour, spooned and leveled

½ tsp baking powder

¼ tsp salt

6 oz (170 g) bar-style milk chocolate, roughly chopped

Preheat the oven to 350°F (175°C). Line two baking sheets with parchment paper and set aside.

In a large bowl, using an electric mixer fitted with a paddle or whisk attachment, mix the butter and both sugars on medium speed just until combined, about 1 minute. Then, add the egg and vanilla and mix for about 30 seconds, or just until combined. Add the flour, baking powder and salt and mix until incorporated, about 1 minute. Then, stir in the chocolate chunks until incorporated.

Scoop 12 equal-sized balls (about 2 to 3 tablespoons [55 to 60 g] each) and place 6 cookies, about 3 inches (7.5 cm) apart, on each prepared baking sheet. Bake one sheet at a time for 10 to 12 minutes, or until the cookies look puffy, pale and dry.

Remove from the oven and let cool on the baking sheet for about 5 minutes, or until firm enough to move. Then, transfer to a wire rack and let cool completely. The cookies will stay fresh in an airtight container at room temperature for up to 4 days or freeze for up to 2 months.

For me, these are classic breakfast cookies. Especially on Saturdays, when Mario and I can sleep in and have an extended brunch after getting up. Enjoying a hearty brunch and finishing it with a couple of these superchewy cookies is just great. I love to reheat mine for about 15 seconds in the microwave and then eat them immediately when they are slightly warm. Don't get me wrong. I don't put all of my cookies in the microwave before I eat them, but with these cookies, it is absolutely delicious. Try it yourself!

Thick Cranberry Oatmeal White Chocolate Chip Cookies

YIELD: **12** COOKIES

½ cup (113 g [1 stick]) unsalted butter, at room temperature

½ cup (100 g) sugar

⅛ cup (25 g) packed light brown sugar

1 large egg

1 tsp vanilla extract

¾ cup (105 g) all-purpose flour, spooned and leveled

½ tsp baking powder

¼ tsp salt

1¼ cups (125 g) old-fashioned rolled oats

1 cup (170 g) white chocolate chips

½ cup (65 g) dried cranberries

Preheat the oven to 350°F (175°C). Line two baking sheets with parchment paper and set aside.

In a large bowl, using an electric mixer fitted with a paddle or whisk attachment, mix the butter and both sugars on medium speed just until combined, about 1 minute. Then, add the egg and vanilla and mix for about 30 seconds, or just until combined. Add the flour, baking powder and salt and mix until incorporated, about 1 minute. Stir in the oats, chocolate chips and cranberries just to incorporate, about 1 minute.

Scoop 12 equal-sized balls (about 2 to 3 tablespoons [65 to 70 g] each) and place 6 cookies, about 3 inches (7.5 cm) apart, on each prepared baking sheet. Bake one sheet at a time for 11 to 13 minutes, or until the cookies look pale, puffy and dry.

Remove from the oven and let cool on the baking sheet for about 5 minutes, or until firm enough to move. Then, transfer to a wire rack and let cool completely. The cookies will stay fresh in an airtight container at room temperature for up to 3 days or freeze for up to 2 months.

NOTE: Replace the cranberries with additional white chocolate chips or either a combination of milk chocolate chips or semisweet chocolate chips, if preferred.

These macarons are just pure joy to eat. Their texture is amazing, and their taste, just out of this world. With my easy-to-follow instructions, you will be able to master this wonderful recipe step by step.

Please note: Because having the correct amount of the ingredients is crucial for the success of this recipe, I suggest you weigh your ingredients in ounces or grams, rather than measure in cups. Cups are fine to bake with most of the time, but with macarons, we need to be very accurate.

Dark Chocolate Mint Macarons

YIELD: 30 MACARONS

MACARONS

4.59 oz (130 g) almond flour

4.59 oz (130 g) powdered sugar

3.53 oz (100 g) egg whites, at room temperature (2 to 3 large eggs)

¼ tsp cream of tartar

3.17 oz (90 g) superfine sugar

¼ tsp peppermint extract

Green gel food coloring (optional)

CHOCOLATE FILLING

4.5 oz (128 g) bar-style semisweet chocolate, finely chopped

3 fl oz (90 ml) heavy cream

¼ tsp peppermint extract

Line two or three baking sheets with parchment paper and set aside, or have ready two or three silicone macaron mats.

Make the macarons: In a medium bowl, sift together the almond flour and powdered sugar twice and set aside.

In a large bowl, using an electric mixer fitted with a whisk attachment, whip the egg whites on medium-low speed until foamy, 3 to 4 minutes. Then, add the cream of tartar and continue to mix for about 1 minute. With the mixer running, add 1 tablespoon (14 g) of superfine sugar at a time while slowly increasing the speed of the mixer, until all the sugar is added, 30 to 60 seconds.

Once all the sugar is incorporated, increase the mixer speed to high and whisk the egg whites until stiff peaks form, 3 to 4 minutes. Add the peppermint extract and the food coloring (if using) in the last minute and mix just until well combined.

Sift about one-third of the almond flour mixture on top of the egg white mixture and gently fold it in until well incorporated. Repeat two more times, until all of the almond flour is combined with the egg whites. Stop folding when the batter falls off your spatula slowly and evenly and you can "draw" a figure eight with the dripping batter. The ribbons should sink into the rest of the batter and completely disappear after 10 seconds. Test the consistency often and stop mixing immediately after reaching that point.

If using parchment paper to line your baking sheets, first spread a dot of batter on each corner of each baking sheet and place the paper on top so that it doesn't move around while you pipe the macarons. Spoon the batter into a large pastry bag fitted with a medium round tip. Pipe 1-inch (2.5-cm) dollops, spaced about 1 inch (2.5 cm) apart, onto the prepared baking sheets or silicone mats.

Firmly but carefully tap the baking sheets on the counter a couple of times to release any air bubbles. Let the macarons sit on the counter for up to 1 hour, or until the surface of the macarons is dry to the touch.

Preheat the oven to 300°F (150°C) and bake one sheet at a time for 17 to 19 minutes, or until the macarons have well risen and they don't stick to the parchment paper anymore.

Remove from the oven, transfer to a wire rack and let cool to room temperature before you fill them.

Make the filling: Place the chocolate in a medium bowl. In a separate microwave-safe bowl, microwave the cream and the peppermint extract together on a medium setting until the mixture starts to simmer, 1 to 2 minutes. Pour the hot cream mixture over the chocolate and let sit for 1 to 2 minutes. Then, stir until the chocolate is completely melted and combined with the cream. Let cool for about 30 minutes, or until firm enough to pipe.

Place the chocolate filling in a piping bag fitted with a tip of your choice (I used a round tip). Add a dollop of filling to a macaron shell and top it, sandwich style, with a second macaron shell. Repeat until all the macaron sandwiches are formed.

Place in an airtight container in the fridge for 24 hours so that the shells get softer and chewy. Be sure to store these cookies in the fridge because the chilling contributes to the chewy signature texture of macarons. I let mine come to room temperature for 15 minutes before I eat them. Store in the fridge for up to 3 days.

*See photo on page 9.

CUPCAKES AND MUFFINS FOR EVERY OCCASION

I enjoy chocolate muffins for breakfast and chocolate cupcakes for dessert—or vice versa. I guarantee you will appreciate all the following cupcake and muffin recipes at any time of the day. They are easy to make, you can prepare them in very little time and they are perfect for every occasion. From office parties to baby showers to family retreats, with chocolate cupcakes and muffins, you will always win the heart of your audience.

In this chapter, we will explore some great combinations, such as pistachio and chocolate (page 65), cherry and chocolate (page 58), caramel apple and chocolate (page 69), orange and chocolate (page 70), strawberry and chocolate (page 62), peanut butter and chocolate (page 61) and of course, chocolate and chocolate (page 66). I'm so happy to share my top-rated chocolate cupcakes and muffins recipes with you!

With this go-to recipe, you can have awesome bakery-style chocolate chip muffins whenever you want them. Although I have a deep affection for delicious bakery treats, nothing beats homemade goodies: You know what is in them and you are emotionally connected because there is a bit of you and your love for baking in every bite. Plus, it's so rewarding to bite into the finished product after making it with your own hands.

Chocolate Chip Streusel Muffins

YIELD: **19** OR **20** MUFFINS

MUFFINS

2 cups (270 g) all-purpose flour, spooned and leveled

2½ tsp (10 g) baking powder

½ tsp salt

¼ tsp ground nutmeg

¼ cup (57 g [½ stick]) unsalted butter, melted

¼ cup (60 ml) vegetable or canola oil

1 cup (200 g) sugar

2 large eggs

1 cup (240 ml) buttermilk

2 tsp (10 ml) vanilla extract

1 cup (170 g) semisweet chocolate chips

STREUSEL

⅜ cup (51 g) all-purpose flour, spooned and leveled

¼ cup (50 g) packed light brown sugar

3 tbsp (43 g) unsalted cold butter, cut into small cubes

Preheat the oven to 425°F (220°C). Line two 12-well muffin pans with about 20 paper liners and set aside.

Make the muffin batter: In a medium bowl, stir together the flour, baking powder, salt and nutmeg and set aside.

In a large bowl, using a whisk, mix together the melted butter, oil and sugar just until combined, about 1 minute. Then, add the eggs, buttermilk and vanilla and stir to combine, about 1 minute. Add the flour mixture and whisk until thoroughly combined, about 1 more minute. Then, fold in the chocolate chips just to incorporate and set aside.

Make the streusel: In a small bowl, use your fingers to combine the flour, brown sugar and butter until the mixture is crumbly. Do not overwork; otherwise, it will become a paste rather than crumbs.

Spoon the batter into the prepared wells until almost full and top with the streusel. You will end up with 19 or 20 muffins. Bake at 425°F (220°C) for 5 minutes. Then, leaving the oven door closed, lower the heat to 350°F (175°C) and bake for another 11 to 13 minutes, or until a toothpick inserted into the center of a muffin comes out clean.

Remove from the oven and let cool completely in the pan or transfer to a wire rack after 15 minutes, before serving. Store in an airtight container at room temperature for up to 3 days or freeze for up to 2 months.

Black Forest Chocolate Cupcakes

YIELD: **16** OR **17** CUPCAKES

CHERRY FILLING

1 cup (175 g) canned sour cherries, drained (¼ cup [60 ml] canned cherry water reserved, divided)

2 tsp (5 g) cornstarch

2 tbsp (30 ml) kirsch

3 tbsp (38 g) sugar

CUPCAKES

⅔ cup (89 g) all-purpose flour, spooned and leveled

⅓ cup (28 g) unsweetened Dutch-processed cocoa powder, spooned and leveled

1½ tsp (6 g) baking powder

½ tsp salt

1 large egg

¾ cup (150 g) sugar

½ cup (120 ml) vegetable or canola oil

1 tsp vanilla extract

½ cup (120 ml) buttermilk

WHIPPED CREAM

1½ cups (360 ml) heavy whipping cream

2 tbsp (25 g) sugar

SERVING SUGGESTIONS

Chocolate shavings and fresh cherries

Make the filling: Chop the drained sour cherries into about ¼-inch (0.6-cm) pieces and set aside. In a separate small bowl, stir together the cornstarch and 2 tablespoons (30 ml) of the canned sour cherry water and set aside.

In a small saucepan over medium heat, bring 2 tablespoons (30 ml) of the canned sour cherry water, kirsch and sugar to a simmer, stirring constantly, 2 to 3 minutes. Once at a simmer, stir in the cornstarch slurry and cook, still stirring, for 1 to 2 minutes, or until the mixture gets thick like syrup and coats the back of a spoon. Then, remove from the heat and pour over the chopped cherries. Let cool to room temperature.

Make the cupcakes: Preheat the oven to 350°F (175°C). Line two 12-well muffin pans with 16 or 17 paper liners and set aside.

In a medium bowl, stir together the flour, cocoa powder, baking powder and salt and set aside.

In a large bowl, using an electric mixer fitted with a whisk or paddle attachment, beat the egg and sugar on medium speed until creamy, about 2 minutes. Then, add the oil and vanilla and stir until smooth, about 1 minute. Alternately add the flour mixture and the buttermilk, beginning and ending with the flour mixture, beating on low speed until just combined, 1 to 2 minutes.

Spoon the batter into the prepared wells until no more than two-thirds to three-quarters full, so that your cupcakes don't sink or spill over the sides. Bake for 17 to 20 minutes, or until a toothpick inserted into the center of a cupcake comes out clean. Remove from the oven and let cool completely in the pan, about 30 minutes.

Make the whipped cream: In a large bowl, using an electric mixer fitted with a whisk attachment, whisk the cream until soft peaks form. Then, add the sugar and whisk until stiff peaks form.

When the cupcakes and the sour cherry filling have cooled, use the back of a piping tip (I used a Wilton 1M tip) or a sharp knife to cut out a hole in the center of all the cupcakes. Then, scoop 1 to 1½ tablespoons (15 to 23 ml) of the sour cherry filling into each cupcake and pipe the whipped cream on top.

If you like, garnish your cupcakes with chocolate shavings and fresh cherries on top. Eat the cupcakes within 2 days and store in the fridge.

These soft, fluffy and moist peanut butter cupcakes are topped with an I-have-no-words-for-it creamy chocolate frosting. These are perfect birthday cupcakes for everybody who loves peanut butter and chocolate. I recommend using creamy peanut butter, not a chunky or all-natural one, as it brings the best results and leads to soft and moist cupcakes. Otherwise, the cupcakes may end up dry and crumbly.

Peanut Butter Cupcakes with Chocolate Frosting

YIELD: **16** OR **17** CUPCAKES

CUPCAKES

1¼ cups (169 g) all-purpose flour, spooned and leveled

2 tsp (8 g) baking powder

¼ tsp salt

½ cup (120 ml) vegetable or canola oil

½ cup (125 g) creamy peanut butter

1 large egg

¾ cup (150 g) packed light brown sugar

1 tsp vanilla extract

1 cup (240 ml) buttermilk

FROSTING

1 cup (226 g [2 sticks]) unsalted butter, at room temperature

¼ cup (63 g) creamy peanut butter

1 tsp vanilla extract

2½ cups (300 g) unpacked powdered sugar

½ cup (43 g) unsweetened natural cocoa powder, spooned and leveled

Pinch of salt

Make the cupcakes: Preheat the oven to 350°F (175°C). Line two 12-well muffin pans with 16 or 17 paper liners and set aside.

In a medium bowl, stir together the flour, baking powder and salt and set aside.

In a large bowl, using an electric mixer fitted with a whisk or paddle attachment, beat the oil, peanut butter, egg, brown sugar and vanilla on medium-low speed just until thoroughly combined, 1 to 2 minutes. Then, alternately add the flour mixture and buttermilk, beginning and ending with the flour mixture, mixing on low speed just to combine, 1 to 2 minutes.

Spoon the batter into the prepared wells until no more than two-thirds to three-quarters full, so that your cupcakes don't sink or spill over the sides. Bake for 17 to 20 minutes, or until a toothpick inserted into the center of a cupcake comes out clean.

Remove from the oven and let cool completely in the pan, about 30 minutes.

Make the frosting: In a large bowl, using an electric mixer fitted with a whisk or paddle attachment, beat the butter on medium-high speed until soft and creamy, 2 to 3 minutes. Add the peanut butter and vanilla and mix to combine, about 1 minute. Gradually add the powdered sugar, cocoa powder and salt and beat on medium-low speed until fully combined, fluffy and smooth, about 2 minutes.

Spoon or pipe the frosting on top of the cupcakes according to your preference (I used a Wilton 8B tip). Store the cupcakes in an airtight container at room temperature for up to 2 days or in the fridge for up to 3 days.

These cupcakes have a special place in my heart because they remind me of my childhood and baking with my mother after picking fresh strawberries. They are topped with irresistibly creamy white chocolate frosting in addition to strawberry frosting. Yes, you read that correctly. The frosting is actually divided into one part white chocolate frosting and one part strawberry frosting. The point isn't to create a two-toned frosting, but to let both flavors stand out on their own. If you want to have a lightly pinkish strawberry frosting, you can add a drop of pink or red gel food coloring.

Supermoist White Chocolate–Strawberry Cupcakes

YIELD: **16** OR **17** CUPCAKES

CUPCAKES

1¼ cups (169 g) all-purpose flour, spooned and leveled

2 tsp (8 g) baking powder

½ tsp salt

1 large egg

½ cup (100 g) sugar

½ cup (120 ml) vegetable oil

3 oz (85 g) bar-style white chocolate, melted and cooled

¼ cup (80 g) strawberry jam

2 tsp (10 ml) vanilla extract

½ cup (120 ml) buttermilk

FROSTING

1 cup (226 g [2 sticks]) unsalted butter, at room temperature

2 cups (240 g) unpacked powdered sugar, sifted

1 tsp vanilla extract

3 oz (85 g) bar-style white chocolate, melted and cooled

¼ cup (80 g) strawberry jam

Make the cupcakes: Preheat the oven to 350°F (175°C). Line two 12-well muffin pans with 16 or 17 paper liners and set aside.

In a medium bowl, stir together the flour, baking powder and salt and set aside.

In a large bowl, using an electric mixer fitted with a whisk or paddle attachment, beat the egg and sugar on medium speed until creamy, about 2 minutes. Then, add the oil, melted chocolate, strawberry jam and vanilla and stir until smooth, about 1 minute. Alternately add the flour mixture and the buttermilk, beginning and ending with the flour mixture, mixing on low speed just until combined, 1 to 2 minutes.

Spoon the batter into the prepared wells until no more than two-thirds to three-quarters full, so that your cupcakes don't sink or spill over the sides. Bake for 17 to 20 minutes, or until a toothpick inserted into the center of a cupcake comes out clean.

Remove from the oven and let cool completely in the pan, about 30 minutes.

Make the frosting: In a large bowl, beat the butter on medium-high speed until soft and creamy, 2 to 3 minutes. Add the powdered sugar and beat on medium-low speed until fully incorporated and smooth, about 2 minutes. Then, stir in the vanilla until combined. Divide the frosting in half and transfer to two medium bowls.

Place the melted chocolate in one of the bowls and the strawberry jam in the other and, using clean beaters, beat each frosting mixture on medium speed until creamy, 1 to 2 minutes.

Spoon the frosting alternately into a piping bag or use a two-tone piping bag to frost the cupcakes. Store the cupcakes in an airtight container in the refrigerator for up to 3 days.

I adore pistachios, so these muffins are my first choice for cozy weekend nights with my hubby. My two favorite munchies combined: pistachios and chocolate. The cream cheese in the batter makes these muffins incredibly moist and soft, and do you see how perfectly domed they are? They are not just delicious; they are also very pretty, don't you think?

Dark Chocolate Pistachio Cream Cheese Muffins

YIELD: 19 OR 20 MUFFINS

MUFFINS

2 cups (270 g) all-purpose flour, spooned and leveled

1 cup (85 g) unsweetened Dutch-processed cocoa powder, spooned and leveled

4 tsp (16 g) baking powder

¼ tsp salt

8 oz (227 g) cream cheese, softened

1 cup (200 g) sugar

1 tsp vanilla extract

2 large eggs

1 cup (240 ml) milk

½ cup (113 g [1 stick]) unsalted butter, melted and cooled

1 cup (130 g) raw, shelled and peeled pistachios, chopped

STREUSEL

⅓ cup (45 g) all-purpose flour, spooned and leveled

2 tbsp (25 g) sugar

3 tbsp (43 g) unsalted cold butter, cut into small cubes

½ cup (65 g) raw peeled pistachios, chopped

Preheat the oven to 425°F (220°C). Line two 12-well muffin pans with about 20 paper liners and set aside.

Make the muffin batter: In a medium bowl, stir together the flour, cocoa powder, baking powder and salt and set aside.

In a large bowl, using an electric mixer fitted with a whisk or paddle attachment, beat the cream cheese, sugar and vanilla on medium speed until creamy and smooth, about 2 minutes. Then, add the eggs, milk and melted butter and mix until smooth and combined, about 1 minute. With the mixer on low speed, slowly mix in the flour mixture, about 1 minute. Do not overmix at any step. Then, fold in the pistachios just to incorporate and set aside.

Make the streusel: In a small bowl, use your fingers to combine the flour, sugar, butter and pistachios until the mixture is crumbly. Do not overwork; otherwise, it will become a paste rather than crumbs.

Spoon the batter into the prepared wells until almost full and top with the streusel. You will end up with 19 or 20 muffins. Bake at 425°F (220°C) for 5 minutes. Then, leaving the oven door closed, lower the heat to 350°F (175°C) and bake for another 11 to 13 minutes, or until a toothpick inserted into the center of a muffin comes out clean.

Remove from the oven and let cool completely in the pan or transfer to a wire rack after 15 minutes, before serving. Store in an airtight container at room temperature for up to 3 days or freeze for up to 2 months.

NOTE: If you want to have a bit of a salty note in your muffins, use salted and roasted pistachios instead of raw ones. Either way, I recommend removing as much skin as possible.

These cupcakes literally scream CHOCOLATE! I mean, imagine a chocolate cupcake filled with chocolate filling. That's the ultimate chocolate lover's cupcake, for sure. These are also a good choice for anyone who loves the taste of coffee in baked goods. Chocolate and coffee just go so well together.

Brooklyn Blackout Chocolate Cupcakes

YIELD: **14** OR **15** CUPCAKES

CUPCAKES

⅔ cup (89 g) all-purpose flour, spooned and leveled

⅓ cup (28 g) unsweetened natural cocoa powder, spooned and leveled

¾ cup (150 g) sugar

¾ tsp baking powder

¼ tsp baking soda

½ tsp salt

1 tsp espresso powder

1 large egg

½ cup (120 ml) vegetable or canola oil

1 tsp vanilla extract

¼ cup (60 ml) buttermilk

¼ cup (60 ml) hot strongly brewed coffee

FILLING

¾ cup (150 g) sugar

1 cup (240 ml) milk

3 oz (85 g) bar-style semisweet chocolate, roughly chopped

3 tbsp (24 g) cornstarch

1 tsp espresso powder

1 tsp vanilla extract

Pinch of salt

Make the cupcakes: Preheat the oven to 350°F (175°C). Line two 12-well muffin pans with 14 or 15 paper liners and set aside.

In a medium bowl, sift together the flour, cocoa powder, sugar, baking powder, baking soda, salt and espresso powder and set aside.

In a large bowl, using an electric mixer fitted with a whisk or paddle attachment, beat the egg, oil, vanilla and buttermilk on medium-low speed just until thoroughly combined, 1 to 2 minutes. Then, add the flour mixture and mix until smooth, about 1 minute. With the mixer on low speed, slowly add the hot coffee and mix just until combined, 1 to 2 minutes.

Spoon the batter into the prepared wells until no more than two-thirds to three-quarters full, so that your cupcakes don't sink or spill over the sides while baking. Bake for 18 to 20 minutes, or until a toothpick inserted into the center of a cupcake comes out clean.

Remove from the oven and let the cupcakes cool completely in the pan, about 30 minutes.

Make the filling: In a medium saucepan over medium heat, combine the sugar, milk, chopped chocolate, cornstarch and espresso powder and bring to a boil, whisking constantly. Cook, still whisking, for 5 to 7 minutes, or until as thick as pudding.

Remove from the heat and whisk in the vanilla and a pinch of salt. Transfer the filling to a bowl and let chill in the fridge for about 3 hours.

When the cupcakes and the filling have cooled, use the back of a piping tip (I used a Wilton 1M tip) or a sharp knife to cut out a hole in the center of all the cupcakes, reserving the removed cupcake crumbs. Then, scoop about 2 tablespoons (30 g) of the filling into each cupcake and top it with the cupcake crumbs. Store the cupcakes in an airtight container in the fridge for up to 3 days.

NOTE: Don't hollow out the cupcakes too much. Otherwise, the sides will get too thin and the cupcakes will be fragile when filled.

Who else loves chocolate caramel apples? If you ever run into me at a state fair, I'll definitely have one of these in my hand. So, why not turn it into a cupcake I can eat anytime! The combination of chocolate applesauce cupcakes and apple caramel buttercream frosting is just dreamy.

Chocolate Caramel Candy Apple Cupcakes

YIELD: 16 OR 17 CUPCAKES

CUPCAKES

⅔ cup (89 g) all-purpose flour, spooned and leveled

⅓ cup (28 g) unsweetened Dutch-processed cocoa powder, spooned and leveled

1½ tsp (6 g) baking powder

½ tsp salt

1 large egg

¾ cup (150 g) sugar

½ cup (145 g) applesauce

1 tsp vanilla extract

½ cup (120 ml) buttermilk

FROSTING

1¼ cups (300 ml) apple juice

¼ cup (50 g) sugar

1 cup (226 g [2 sticks]) unsalted butter, at room temperature

2 cups (240 g) unpacked powdered sugar, sifted

2 tsp (10 ml) vanilla extract

¼ cup (75 g) caramel sauce

Make the cupcakes: Preheat the oven to 350°F (175°C). Line two 12-well muffin pans with 16 or 17 paper liners and set aside.

In a medium bowl, stir together the flour, cocoa powder, baking powder and salt and set aside.

In a large bowl, using an electric mixer fitted with a whisk or paddle attachment, beat the egg and granulated sugar on medium speed until creamy, about 2 minutes. Then, add the applesauce and vanilla and mix until smooth, about 1 minute. Alternately add the flour mixture and the buttermilk, beginning and ending with the flour mixture, mixing on low speed just until combined, 1 to 2 minutes.

Spoon the batter into the prepared wells until no more than two-thirds to three-quarters full, so that your cupcakes don't sink or spill over the sides. Bake for 17 to 20 minutes, or until a toothpick inserted into the center of a cupcake comes out clean. Remove from the oven and let cool completely in the pan, about 30 minutes.

Make the frosting: In a medium saucepan over medium-high heat, whisk together the apple juice and sugar and bring to a boil. Cook for about 10 minutes, or until reduced by half into a thick syrup. Remove from the heat and let cool completely. The syrup will thicken as it cools; the consistency once cooled should be like honey or caramel syrup.

In a large bowl, beat the butter on medium-high speed until soft and creamy, 2 to 3 minutes. Add the powdered sugar and beat on medium-low speed until fully incorporated and smooth, about 2 minutes. Then, stir in the vanilla until combined. Add the cooled apple juice syrup and caramel sauce and mix on medium speed until combined and creamy, 1 to 2 minutes.

Spoon or pipe the frosting on top of the cupcakes. Store in an airtight container in the refrigerator for up to 2 days.

NOTE: If you accidentally overcooked the apple juice syrup and it is too firm once it cooled, then add fresh apple juice a little at a time and stir until the syrup reaches the right consistency.

Don't these muffins look like little rays of sunshine? They are a dream for every white chocolate lover. To make sure you get your white chocolate fix, I added melted white chocolate to the muffin batter and also white chocolate chips and then candied orange for a crazy-delicious combination. You're going to love these muffins!

White Chocolate Muffins with Candied Orange

YIELD: **18** OR **19** MUFFINS

CANDIED ORANGES

Nonstick spray, for pan

1 medium orange, sliced into ¼" (6-mm) slices

½ cup (100 g) sugar

Juice of ½ orange

MUFFINS

2 cups (270 g) all-purpose flour, spooned and leveled

¾ cup (150 g) sugar

1 tbsp (12 g) baking powder

½ tsp salt

1 large egg

1 cup (240 ml) buttermilk

½ cup (120 ml) vegetable or canola oil

1 tsp vanilla extract

3 oz (85 g) bar-style white chocolate, melted and cooled

½ cup (170 g) white chocolate chunks or chips

Make the candied oranges: Spray a parchment paper–lined baking sheet liberally with nonstick spray and set aside.

In a large skillet over medium-high heat, combine the orange slices, sugar and orange juice and bring to a boil. Cook, stirring regularly, until the orange slices are translucent, 5 to 10 minutes.

Transfer the orange slices, in a single layer, to the prepared baking sheet and let them cool and dry for about 30 minutes. Do not overlap the slices; otherwise, they will stick together once dry. Cut the slices into 18 or 19 quarters and the rest into ¼-inch (6-mm) pieces and set aside.

Make the muffins: Preheat the oven to 425°F (220°C). Line two 12-well muffin pans with 18 or 19 paper liners and set aside.

In a medium bowl, stir together the flour, sugar, baking powder and salt and set aside. In a large bowl, whisk together the egg, buttermilk, oil and vanilla to combine, about 1 minute. Then, add the melted chocolate and whisk to incorporate, another minute. Stir in the flour mixture just to combine, about 1 more minute. Then, fold in the chocolate chunks and the orange pieces just to combine.

Spoon the batter into the prepared wells until almost full and top with the quartered orange slices. You will end up with 18 or 19 muffins. Bake the muffins at 425°F (220°C) for 5 minutes. Then, leaving the oven door closed, lower the heat to 350°F (175°C) and bake for another 12 to 14 minutes, or until a toothpick inserted into the center of a muffin comes out clean.

Remove from the oven and let the muffins cool completely in the pan or transfer to a wire rack after 15 minutes, before serving. Store the muffins in an airtight container at room temperature for up to 3 days or freeze for up to 1 month.

NOTE: Make sure to liberally grease the parchment paper and also the tip of the tool that you use for the candied orange slices so they don't stick to the paper when they dry.

CRAVE-WORTHY CAKES

Chocolate cakes are very popular for a good reason. They come in all sizes and shapes, and there is a chocolate cake recipe for every occasion and season. I'm a chocolate cake person myself, and it was very hard to pick only a couple of all the amazing cake recipes out there. But I'm more than happy to share my all-time favorite and foolproof recipes with you in this chapter. You will find a broad variety from a jaw-dropping 6-layer chocolate cake, to a quick and easy chocolate loaf cake, to mini chocolate cakes that will bring every chocolate lover to their knees.

This chapter contains everyday and down-to-earth chocolate cake recipes, creative recipes for special occasions and chocolate classics with a twist. I went a little crazy with the flavors, so be prepared to see unusual but delicious combinations like lemon and poppyseed with white chocolate or even Thai chilies, which make their appearance in this chapter. There will be THE perfect chocolate cake recipe for everyone.

I wish I had a birthday 365 days a year to have an excuse to eat this ultimate chocolate layer cake every day. It's so dreamy and extremely chocolaty—a chocolate fanatic's dream birthday cake. My family requests this soft and moist dessert, its six cake layers filled and frosted with creamy chocolate buttercream frosting, for almost every birthday. Although I explain how to store leftovers, trust me, there will hardly ever be any extra slices left! Oh, and please don't think you're just allowed to bake this beauty when somebody has a birthday. It's an all-year-round chocolate cake for every occasion, from my go-to basic chocolate cake recipe.

Mind-Blowing Chocolate Fudge Birthday Layer Cake

YIELD: 16 SERVINGS

CAKE

Nonstick spray, for pans

2½ cups (338 g) all-purpose flour, spooned and leveled

1¼ cups (106 g) unsweetened Dutch-processed cocoa powder, spooned and leveled

2¼ cups (450 g) sugar

1 tbsp (12 g) baking powder

1½ tsp (9 g) salt

1½ tsp (3 g) espresso powder (optional)

3 large eggs

¾ cup (180 ml) vegetable or canola oil

¾ cup (180 ml) buttermilk

2 tsp (10 ml) vanilla extract

6 oz (170 g) bar-style semisweet chocolate, melted

1½ cups (360 ml) boiling water

Make the cake: Preheat the oven to 350°F (175°C). Line three 8-inch (20-cm) round baking pans by cutting parchment paper into a circle for the bottom of each pan and a long strip for the sides of each pan, spraying a bit of nonstick spray underneath the papers to make them stick. Set aside.

In a medium bowl, sift together the flour, cocoa powder, sugar, baking powder, salt and espresso powder (if using) and set aside.

In a large bowl, using an electric mixer fitted with a whisk or paddle attachment, mix the eggs, oil, buttermilk and vanilla on medium-low speed just until combined, about 1 minute. Then, add the flour mixture and mix until well combined, about 1 minute. Stir in the melted chocolate and mix just until incorporated, about 1 minute. Then, slowly mix in the hot water until combined, about 1 minute.

Divide the batter equally among the three prepared pans and spread to even the tops. Bake for 20 to 22 minutes, or until a toothpick inserted into the center comes out clean.

Remove from the oven and let cool in the pans for about 20 minutes. Then, transfer to a wire rack and let cool completely, 1 to 2 hours.

When cooled, using a long, sharp knife, cut off the top of each cake layer to create an even surface, if necessary. Then, cut each cake layer in half horizontally and set aside.

(Continued)

Mind-Blowing Chocolate Fudge Birthday Layer Cake (Continued)

FROSTING

2¼ cups (509 g [4½ sticks]) unsalted butter, at room temperature

4¼ cups (510 g) unpacked powdered sugar

¼ cup (21 g) unsweetened natural cocoa powder, spooned and leveled

13.5 oz (383 g) bar-style semisweet chocolate, melted and cooled

Make the frosting: In a large bowl, using an electric mixer fitted with a whisk or paddle attachment, beat the butter until fluffy and creamy, about 2 minutes. Then, sift in the powdered sugar and cocoa powder and whisk until creamy and combined, about 2 minutes. Add the melted chocolate and stir until well incorporated and smooth, about 2 minutes.

Place one cake layer on a cake stand or cake turner and evenly spread one-seventh of the frosting on top. This works best with an offset spatula. Then, place a second cake layer on top and repeat the process. Continue until five of the six cake layers are assembled. Then, place the last cake layer on top, and spread the remaining frosting on top and around the sides, to lightly frost the outside of the cake.

Let chill in the fridge for 4 hours, then slice the cake and serve. Store in an airtight container in the fridge for up to 4 days or freeze for up to 2 months.

NOTES: It's also possible to make a three-layer cake. To do so, do not cut the cake layers in half horizontally after cooling.

It's optional to add the espresso powder to the cake batter. However, it enhances and deepens the chocolate flavor. The amount of espresso powder is so little that you won't taste the coffee at all. It's highly recommended, though not necessary if you don't want to add it. The cake is chocolaty and delicious either way.

Hummingbird cake is a true southern classic and always fulfills expectations. But is it actually possible to make it even better? Yes . . . with chocolate. Chocolate makes everything better! This cake is just awesome, with white chocolate cream cheese frosting and a supershiny white chocolate ganache, with the addition of banana, pineapple and pecans. The cake layers themselves feature a little bit of cocoa powder to enhance and support the chocolate flavor even more. It's a beautiful cake and suitable for special occasions because of its presentation. But, trust me, it tastes even better than it looks.

Show-Stopping Hummingbird White Chocolate Drip Cake

YIELD: **16** SERVINGS

CAKE

2 cups (220 g) pecans, divided

Nonstick spray, for pans

3 cups (405 g) all-purpose flour, spooned and leveled

2 tbsp (11 g) unsweetened natural cocoa powder

1 tsp baking powder

1 tsp baking soda

1 tsp ground cinnamon

½ tsp salt

3 large eggs

1 cup (240 ml) vegetable or canola oil

1¾ cups (350 g) sugar

2 cups (470 g) mashed bananas (4 to 5 medium bananas)

1 (8-oz [227-g]) can crushed pineapple, undrained

2 tsp (10 ml) vanilla extract

Make the cake: Preheat the oven to 300°F (150°C). Spread out the pecans on a parchment paper–lined baking sheet and toast for 8 minutes. Remove from the oven and let cool for 15 minutes. Then, roughly chop and set aside.

Increase the oven temperature to 350°F (175°C). Line three 8-inch (20-cm) round baking pans by cutting parchment paper into a circle for the bottom of each pan and a long strip for the sides of each pan, spraying a bit of nonstick spray underneath the paper to stick it to the pans. Set aside.

In a medium bowl, whisk together the flour, cocoa powder, baking powder, baking soda, cinnamon and salt and set aside.

In a large bowl, whisk the eggs, oil, sugar, bananas, undrained pineapple and vanilla until just combined, about 1 minute. Add the flour mixture and whisk just to combine, about 1 minute. Whisk in 1½ cups (165 g) of the toasted pecans until they are evenly distributed throughout the cake batter.

Divide the batter equally among the three prepared pans and spread to even the batter. Bake for 26 to 30 minutes, or until a toothpick inserted into the center of a layer comes out clean.

Remove from the oven and let cool in the pans for 15 to 20 minutes. Then, transfer to a wire rack and let cool completely, 1 to 2 hours.

Use a long, sharp knife to cut off the top of each cake layer to create an even surface, if necessary. Set aside.

(Continued)

Show-Stopping Hummingbird White Chocolate Drip Cake (Continued)

FROSTING

1 cup (226 g [2 sticks]) unsalted butter, at room temperature

8 oz (227 g) cream cheese, softened

8 oz (227 g) bar-style white chocolate, melted and cooled

1 tsp vanilla extract

2 cups (240 g) unpacked powdered sugar

GANACHE

6 oz (170 g) bar-style white chocolate, finely chopped

⅓ cup (80 ml) heavy whipping cream

Make the frosting: In a large bowl, using an electric mixer fitted with a whisk or paddle attachment, beat the butter and cream cheese until fluffy and creamy, 2 to 3 minutes. Add the melted chocolate and vanilla and stir until well combined and smooth, about 2 minutes. Then, sift in the powdered sugar and whisk until incorporated, about 2 minutes.

Place one cake layer on a cake stand or cake turner and evenly spread one-third of the frosting on top. This works best with an offset spatula. Place another cake layer on top and repeat the process. Then, place the third cake layer on top and spread the remaining frosting on top and around the sides to lightly frost the outside of the cake. Let the cake chill in the fridge for 4 hours.

Make the ganache: Place the chocolate in a heatproof bowl and set aside. In a microwave-safe bowl, microwave the cream on a medium setting until it reaches a simmer, 1 to 2 minutes. Then, pour the cream over the chocolate and let sit for 2 minutes. Stir until the chocolate is completely melted and the ganache is smooth.

Slowly and smoothly pour the ganache on top of the chilled cake in a circular motion, starting in the center and moving outward to the edges. Using a cake turner makes this easier. Let the ganache drip down the sides of the cake. Then, top with the remaining toasted pecans and chill the cake for 1 hour in the refrigerator.

Slice the chilled cake and serve. Store in an airtight container in the fridge for up to 4 days or freeze for up to 1 month.

NOTE: The cocoa powder in the cake is just to support the chocolate flavor of the cake overall and is not very present on its own.

Starting to add freshly chopped banana to my chocolate banana loaf cake changed everything. The soft chunks throughout this otherwise already perfectly moist, soft and flavorful loaf cake brings this recipe to the next level. It's a game-changer; I mean it. We typically enjoy this cake for weekend brunch and everyone raves over it.

Chocolate Banana Loaf Cake

YIELD: **12** SERVINGS

1⅓ cups (180 g) all-purpose flour, spooned and leveled

½ cup (43 g) unsweetened natural cocoa powder, spooned and leveled

1 tsp baking powder

¼ tsp baking soda

Pinch of salt

1⅔ cups (390 g) mashed very ripe bananas (3 to 4 medium bananas)

¾ cup (150 g) sugar

½ cup (120 ml) vegetable or canola oil

2 large eggs

2 tsp (10 ml) vanilla extract

¾ cup (128 g) semisweet chocolate chips

2 medium bananas, chopped

Optional topping: 1 banana, cut in half lengthwise, plus 2 tbsp (21 g) semisweet chocolate chips

Preheat the oven to 350°F (175°C). Line a 9 x 5-inch (23 x 13-cm) loaf pan with parchment paper with an overhang around the edges and set aside.

In a small bowl, stir together the flour, cocoa, baking powder, baking soda and salt and set aside.

In a large bowl, whisk together the mashed bananas and sugar just until combined, about 1 minute. Then, slowly whisk in the oil just to combine, another minute. Add the eggs and vanilla and stir just to combine, about 1 minute. Then, add the flour mixture and whisk just until combined, another 1 minute. Fold in the chocolate chips and chopped banana and transfer the batter to the prepared pan.

Top the batter with the halved banana and additional chocolate chips, if desired. Bake for 60 to 70 minutes, or until a toothpick inserted into the center comes out clean.

Remove the bread from the oven and let cool in the pan for about 15 minutes. Then, use the parchment to lift the bread from the pan. Transfer to a wire rack to cool completely. Store in an airtight container at room temperature for up to 3 days or freeze for up to 1 month.

NOTE: If you don't have very ripe bananas at hand, mash firmer bananas and combine with 1 tablespoon (15 ml) of pure maple syrup to get the same sweetness and soft texture.

There are so many things I love about this cake: It is fluffy, moist and soft, and the peanut butter is the perfect addition! Personally, I love that the peanut butter is concentrated in one place rather than swirled throughout the cake, but it's up to you. You definitely can spoon the chocolate and peanut butter alternately into the pan to distribute them more evenly, making sure that the bottom of your pan is fully covered with chocolate batter before you add the peanut butter swirl because the swirl will sink as it bakes.

Chocolate Peanut Butter Bundt Cake

YIELD: **16** SERVINGS

CAKE

Unsalted butter, for pan

2¼ cups (304 g) all-purpose flour, spooned and leveled, plus more for pan

½ cup (43 g) unsweetened natural cocoa powder, spooned and leveled

1 tsp baking powder

1 tsp baking soda

1 tsp salt

1 tsp espresso powder (optional)

1 cup (226 g [2 sticks]) unsalted butter, at room temperature

1¾ cups (350 g) sugar

2 large eggs

1 tsp vanilla extract

1½ cups (360 ml) milk

SWIRL

1 cup (250 g) creamy peanut butter

⅓ cup (40 g) unpacked powdered sugar

¼ cup (57 g [½ stick]) unsalted butter, melted

1 tsp vanilla extract

⅛ tsp salt

GANACHE

¾ cup (128 g) semisweet chocolate, finely chopped

⅜ cup (90 ml) heavy whipping cream

Preheat the oven to 350°F (175°C). Butter and flour a 10-inch (25-cm) Bundt pan and set aside.

Make the cake batter: In a medium bowl, sift together the flour, cocoa powder, baking powder, baking soda, salt and espresso powder (if using), and set aside.

In a large bowl, using an electric mixer fitted with a whisk or paddle attachment, cream together the softened butter and granulated sugar on medium speed until fluffy and creamy, about 2 minutes. Add the eggs, one at a time, and mix until incorporated, about 1 minute, adding the vanilla along with the second egg. Then, alternately add the flour mixture and milk, beginning and ending with the flour mixture, and stir just until combined. Set aside.

Make the swirl: In a medium bowl, whisk together the peanut butter, powdered sugar, melted butter, vanilla and salt until combined and creamy, 1 to 2 minutes.

Spoon one-half to two-thirds of the chocolate batter into the prepared pan and spoon the peanut butter swirl evenly on top. Top with the remaining chocolate batter. Bake for 55 to 65 minutes, or until a toothpick inserted into the center comes out clean. Remove from the oven and let the cake cool in the pan for 1 hour. Once cool, invert the cake onto a wire rack or plate and let cool completely.

Make the ganache: Place the chopped chocolate in a heatproof bowl and set aside. In a microwave-safe bowl, microwave the cream on a medium setting until it starts to simmer, about 1 minute. Pour the cream over the chocolate and let sit for 2 minutes. Then, stir until the chocolate is completely melted and the ganache is smooth.

Drizzle the ganache on top of your Bundt cake and let dry for 1 hour. Then, cut the cake into slices and serve. Store in an airtight container at room temperature for up to 4 days or freeze without ganache for up to 2 months.

This is hands down the best flourless chocolate cake you will ever have. It's over-the-moon rich, rich, rich! Eating it is like taking a bite of warm, soft, pure chocolate. And the good thing is that even your gluten-intolerant friends and family can enjoy it, since it's completely free of flour or any other gluten product.

Flourless Chocolate Cake

YIELD: **12** SERVINGS

Nonstick spray, for pan

6 oz (170 g) bar-style semisweet chocolate, finely chopped

10 tbsp (142 g) unsalted butter

1 cup (200 g) sugar

2 tsp (10 ml) vanilla extract

¼ tsp salt

4 large eggs

½ cup (43 g) unsweetened Dutch-processed cocoa powder, spooned and leveled

SERVING SUGGESTIONS

Whipped cream, ice cream, berries, and powdered sugar

Preheat the oven to 350°F (175°C). Line the bottom and sides of a 9-inch (23-cm) springform pan by cutting out a circle of parchment paper for the bottom and a long strip for the sides, spraying a bit of nonstick spray underneath the paper to stick it to the pan. Set aside.

In a microwave-safe bowl, combine the chocolate and butter and microwave on a medium setting, stirring every 20 seconds, for 1 to 2 minutes, or until the chocolate is completely melted and combined with the butter.

Transfer the chocolate mixture to a large bowl. Add the sugar, vanilla and salt and whisk just to combine, about 1 minute. Then, whisk in the eggs just until combined, about 1 minute. Sift in the cocoa powder and whisk just to incorporate, about 1 minute.

Pour the batter into the prepared baking pan and bake for 25 to 30 minutes. A toothpick inserted into the center should come out clean with a few moist crumbs.

Remove from the oven and let the cake cool for about 15 minutes. Serve the cake either warm and fresh with some whipped cream, ice cream or fruit on top, or cold with a bit of powdered sugar. Store in an airtight container at room temperature for up to 5 days. Reheat leftover cake slices in the microwave, if desired.

NOTE: Cut the cake slices in one motion with a long, very sharp knife to create the cleanest cuts of the warm chocolate cake. Clean the knife between the cuts.

Lovers' White Chocolate Strawberry Champagne Poke Cake

YIELD: **15** SERVINGS

CAKE

2 cups (270 g) all-purpose flour, spooned and leveled

1 tbsp (12 g) baking powder

½ tsp salt

½ cup (113 g [1 stick]) unsalted butter, at room temperature

½ cup (120 ml) vegetable or canola oil

1 cup (200 g) sugar

2 large eggs

2 tsp (10 ml) vanilla extract

½ cup (120 ml) milk

½ cup (120 ml) high-quality champagne

9 oz (255 g) bar-style white chocolate, melted and cooled

SAUCE

3 cups (450 g) fresh strawberries, hulled

½ cup (120 ml) high-quality champagne

½ cup (100 g) sugar

2 tbsp (16 g) cornstarch

Make the cake: Preheat the oven to 350°F (175°C). Line a 9 x 13-inch (23 x 33–cm) baking pan with parchment paper and set aside.

In a medium bowl, whisk together the flour, baking powder and salt and set aside.

In a large bowl, using an electric mixer fitted with a whisk or paddle attachment, beat the butter, oil and sugar on medium-high speed until creamy and fluffy, 2 to 3 minutes. Add the eggs and vanilla and mix until fully incorporated, about 1 minute. Alternately add the flour mixture, milk and champagne, beginning and ending with the flour mixture, and whisk to combine, about 1 minute. Then, add the melted chocolate and stir to incorporate, about 1 minute.

Transfer the batter to the prepared baking pan and bake for 25 to 30 minutes, or until a toothpick inserted into the center comes out clean.

Remove from the oven and let cool in the pan for about 1 hour.

Make the sauce: In a heavy-bottomed saucepan over medium-high heat, combine the strawberries, champagne, sugar and cornstarch and bring to a boil. Cook until the strawberries are soft, 4 to 5 minutes. Then, mash or puree the strawberries and cook for another 3 to 4 minutes.

Remove the pot from the heat and let the sauce cool for 10 minutes. Then, spacing your pokes 1 inch (2.5 cm) apart, poke the top of the cake halfway through to the bottom, using the handle of a wooden spoon. Pour the sauce evenly over the top of the cake. Let the cake cool and the sauce soak in, for 1 hour.

(Continued)

Lovers' White Chocolate Strawberry Champagne Poke Cake (Continued)

FROSTING

6 oz (170 g) bar-style white chocolate, finely chopped

1½ cups (360 ml) heavy whipping cream, divided

2 tbsp (30 ml) high-quality champagne

SERVING SUGGESTIONS

Fresh strawberries and champagne

Make the frosting: Place the chocolate in a heatproof bowl and set aside. In a microwave-safe bowl, combine ¼ cup (60 ml) of the cream and the champagne and microwave on a medium setting for 1 to 2 minutes, or until the mixture starts to reach a simmer. Pour the hot liquid over the chocolate and let stand for 2 minutes. Then, stir until the chocolate is completely melted and the ganache is smooth. Transfer the ganache to a large bowl and let cool for 10 minutes.

In another large bowl, using an electric mixer fitted with a whisk attachment, whip the remaining 1¼ cups (300 ml) of the cream on medium-high speed until stiff peaks form, 3 to 4 minutes. Gently fold the whipped cream into the chocolate ganache just until combined.

Spread the frosting evenly on top of the cooled cake and chill in the refrigerator for 4 hours or overnight. Slice the chilled cake and serve it with fresh strawberries and champagne, if desired. Store in an airtight container in the fridge for up to 3 days.

NOTE: I mashed the strawberries in the sauce because I love to have some soft strawberry pieces in my cake. If you prefer a smoother sauce, I recommend pureeing the strawberries.

I bake this cake often when the days are getting shorter and fall is all around us. It's such a cozy autumn cake. Picture yourself with a warm slice of this soft, moist chocolate cake that has juicy pears in the center. The syrup adds that extra something-something. Snuggle yourself on the couch under a warming blanket and enjoy it with a huge cup of Earl Grey tea as you look outside the window where it's foggy, windy and rainy.

Earl Grey Chai–Poached Pears Dark Chocolate Cake

YIELD: **8** SERVINGS

PEARS

8 Bosc pears, peeled but left whole

10 cups (2.4 L) water

1 cup (200 g) sugar

4 Earl Grey black tea bags

6 green cardamom pods, crushed

4 allspice berries, crushed

4 cloves

3 cinnamon sticks

2 vanilla pods, split

1 star anise pod

1 thumb-sized piece fresh ginger

½ tsp ground nutmeg

CAKE

Nonstick spray, for pan

1¾ cups (236 g) all-purpose flour, spooned and leveled

¾ cup (64 g) unsweetened natural cocoa powder, spooned and leveled

1½ cups (300 g) sugar

1 tsp baking powder

½ tsp baking soda

1 tsp salt

2 large eggs

½ cup (113 g [1 stick]) unsalted butter, melted

1 cup (240 ml) buttermilk

½ cup (120 ml) reserved cooked pear water

1 tsp vanilla extract

Make the pears: In a large stockpot over medium-high heat, combine all the pears ingredients and bring to a boil. Cook for 15 to 20 minutes, or until the pears are softened but not mushy. Remove 2½ cups (600 ml) of pear water and pour it through a mesh strainer to filter out the spices, then set aside. Discard the rest of the water. Place the pears on a plate and let cool for 15 minutes. Then, cut a small slice off the bottom of each pear so that the bottom is flat and the pear can stand upright.

Make the cake: Preheat the oven to 350°F (175°C). Line the bottom and sides of a 9-inch (23-cm) springform pan with parchment paper, by cutting a circle for the bottom plus a long strip for the sides, spraying a bit of nonstick spray underneath the paper to stick it to the pan. Set aside.

In a medium bowl, sift together the flour, cocoa powder, sugar, baking powder, baking soda and salt and set aside.

In a large bowl, whisk together the eggs, melted butter, buttermilk, ½ cup (120 ml) of the reserved cooked pear water and the vanilla until combined, about 1 minute. Then, add the flour mixture and whisk just to incorporate, about 1 minute.

(Continued)

Earl Grey Chai–Poached Pears Dark Chocolate Cake (Continued)

2 cups (480 ml) reserved cooked pear water

¼ cup (50 g) sugar

Arrange the pears in the pan so that they stand upright. Pour the batter into the pan around the pears. Place in the oven with a piece of parchment paper underneath the pan to prevent any leaking liquid from dripping into the oven. Bake for 45 to 50 minutes, or until a toothpick inserted into the center comes out clean (poke into the cake and not into a pear, to test).

Remove from the oven and let cool for 30 minutes in the pan.

Make the syrup: In a medium saucepan over medium-high heat, combine the remaining 2 cups (480 ml) of reserved cooked pear water and the sugar and bring to a boil. Simmer for 5 to 10 minutes, or until the liquid is reduced by two-thirds. The consistency should be that of caramel syrup.

Spoon the syrup on top of the warm cake. Then, cut the cake into slices and serve while still warm. Store in an airtight container in the fridge for up to 2 days. Reheat the chilled cake in the microwave for 20 to 30 seconds before serving.

NOTE: If you don't want the core of the pears in your cake, carefully remove the core from each pear before you cook them.

There are hardly enough words to describe how awesome this cake is! It is basically a giant chewy, triple-decker cardamom chocolate chip cookie tower, frosted with a heavenly fluffy marshmallow buttercream frosting and additional chocolate chips. It's ridiculously easy to make and definitely a showstopper for every occasion.

Cardamom Chocolate Chip Cookie Layer Cake

YIELD: **16** SERVINGS

CAKE

Nonstick spray, for pans

1½ cups (339 g [3 sticks]) unsalted butter, at room temperature

1 cup (200 g) packed light brown sugar

1 cup (200 g) sugar

2 large eggs

1 tbsp (15 ml) vanilla extract

4 cups (540 g) all-purpose flour, spooned and leveled

1 tbsp (8 g) cornstarch

2 tsp (10 g) baking soda

1 tsp salt

1 tsp ground cardamom

2½ cups (425 g) semisweet chocolate chips

FROSTING

1½ cups (339 g [3 sticks]) unsalted butter, at room temperature

3 cups (360 g) unpacked powdered sugar

2 (14-oz [397-g]) jars marshmallow fluff

1 cup (170 g) semisweet chocolate chips

Make the cake: Preheat the oven to 350°F (175°C). Line three 8-inch (20-cm) round baking pans by cutting parchment paper into a circle for the bottom of each pan and a long strip for the sides of each pan, spraying a bit of nonstick spray underneath the paper to stick it to the pan. Set aside.

In a large bowl, using an electric mixer fitted with a whisk or paddle attachment, beat the butter and both sugars on medium speed until creamy, about 2 minutes. Add the eggs and vanilla and beat to combine, about 1 minute. Then, add the flour, cornstarch, baking soda, salt and cardamom and mix until incorporated, about 1 minute. The batter will be very thick, like cookie dough. Stir in the chocolate chips until evenly distributed throughout the batter.

Divide the batter equally among the three prepared pans and spread to even the tops. Bake for 16 to 18 minutes, or until the tops are golden brown.

Remove from the oven and let cool in the pans for about 20 minutes. Then, transfer to a wire rack and let cool completely, 1 to 2 hours.

Make the frosting: In a large bowl, using an electric mixer fitted with a whisk or paddle attachment, beat the butter until fluffy and creamy, about 2 minutes. Then, sift in the powdered sugar and whisk until creamy and combined, about 2 minutes. Add the marshmallow fluff and stir until well incorporated and smooth, about 2 minutes.

Place 1 cake layer on a cake stand or cake turner and evenly spread one-third of the frosting on top. This works best with an offset spatula. Then, sprinkle with one-third of the chocolate chips. Place another cake layer on top and repeat the process. Then, place the last cake layer on top, spread the remaining frosting on top and sprinkle with the remaining chocolate chips.

Let the cake chill in the fridge for 2 hours. It is easier to slice the cake when the frosting is cold and firm. Store in an airtight container at room temperature for up to 3 days.

I just love chocolate cheesecake! I'm very happy to share my all-time favorite which steals the show from every other cheesecake. If you aren't a big raspberry fan, feel free to top with any other berries you like or skip the berries altogether. It's an incredibly delicious white chocolate cheesecake, either way.

Ultracreamy White Chocolate–Raspberry Cheesecake

YIELD: **12** SERVINGS

Nonstick spray, for pan

CRUST

2½ cups (250 g) graham cracker crumbs, spooned and leveled

2 tbsp (25 g) sugar

¼ cup (57 g [½ stick]) unsalted butter, melted

FILLING

2 lbs (907 g) cream cheese, softened

1 cup (200 g) sugar

2 tbsp (17 g) all-purpose flour

10.5 oz (298 g) bar-style white chocolate, melted and cooled

2 tsp (10 ml) vanilla extract

¼ tsp salt

5 large eggs

⅓ cup (80 ml) heavy whipping cream

2 cups (250 g) fresh raspberries

Preheat the oven to 350°F (175°C). Line the bottom and sides of a 9-inch (23-cm) springform pan with parchment paper. Set aside.

Make the crust: In a medium bowl, combine the graham cracker crumbs, sugar and melted butter and stir until the crumbs are evenly moist. Then, transfer the crumbs to the prepared pan and press the crust into the bottom and halfway up the sides, using the base of a flat-bottomed cup. Bake for 10 minutes. Leaving the oven on, remove the crust from the oven and let cool until ready to fill.

Make the filling: In a large bowl, using an electric mixer fitted with a whisk or paddle attachment, beat the cream cheese, sugar and flour just until combined and no lumps remain. Add the melted chocolate, vanilla and salt and stir just to combine, 30 to 60 seconds. Then, add the eggs, one at a time, and mix just until incorporated, about 15 to 20 seconds after each egg. Scrape down the bowl and add the cream. Mix just to combine, 30 to 60 seconds. Do not overmix at any step.

Pour the filling into the prebaked crust and spread evenly. Scatter the raspberries evenly on top. Place in the oven with a piece of parchment paper underneath the pan to catch any leaking liquid. Bake for 45 to 55 minutes, or until the edges are puffed and set.

Turn off the oven when the center is not yet browned from baking and is almost set with a 4-inch (10-cm) wobbly spot in the center. The cheesecake will get firm as it cools. Propping open the oven door slightly with the handle of a wooden spoon, let the cheesecake sit for another hour in the oven. Then, remove it from the oven and let it cool to room temperature, for about 2 hours.

Once cooled, refrigerate the cake overnight for at least 8 hours. Before serving, remove the cheesecake from the pan and remove the parchment paper, then cut and serve. Store in an airtight container in the refrigerator for up to 3 days.

I recommend freezing leftover cheesecake without the raspberries on top because they get mushy while thawing. The cheesecake itself freezes well for up to 2 months.

Since crepes are usually eaten for breakfast, does that mean that this cake is technically a breakfast cake? Well, you definitely can enjoy this 47-layer dream cake for breakfast, but also for brunch, lunch, dinner, dessert or all day long. This miracle cake has 24 layers of thin chocolate crepes, 12 layers of chocolate whipping cream and 11 layers of apricot jam. It is unique and fun to eat. I decided to go with an apricot jam since it goes so well with dark chocolate. But, of course, you could smear any kind of jam between the crepes.

Dreamy Chocolate-Apricot Crepe Cake

YIELD: **12** SERVINGS

CREPES

6 large eggs

3 cups (720 ml) milk

⅓ cup (75 g) unsalted butter, melted, plus about 1 tbsp (14 g) for pan

1 tsp vanilla extract

2 cups (270 g) all-purpose flour, spooned and leveled

½ cup (43 g) unsweetened Dutch-processed cocoa powder, spooned and leveled

⅓ cup (67 g) sugar

¼ tsp salt

FILLING

2 cups (480 ml) heavy whipping cream

2 tbsp (15 g) powdered sugar

1 tbsp (5 g) unsweetened Dutch-processed cocoa powder

1 cup (300 g) apricot jam

SERVING SUGGESTIONS

Whipped cream and chocolate shavings

Make the crepes: In a blender, combine all the crepe ingredients and blend until the batter is smooth and no lumps remain. Then, let it sit for 2 to 3 minutes.

Heat an 8-inch (20-cm) skillet over medium heat. Lightly butter the pan and spoon about ¼ cup (60 ml) of batter into the pan. Quickly swirl the pan around so that its bottom is thinly and completely covered with crepe batter on the bottom. Cook for about 2 minutes, or until bubbles form on the surface and the crepe is dry enough to not stick to the pan anymore. Flip the crepe and cook on the other side until it doesn't stick to the pan anymore, 2 minutes.

Transfer the crepe to a plate. Repeat, cooking the crepes until you run out of batter. I got 24 crepes. Let the crepes cool completely to room temperature, about 1 hour.

Make the filling: In a large bowl, using an electric mixer fitted with a whisk attachment, whisk the cream on medium-high speed until soft peaks form, about 2 minutes. Then, add the powdered sugar and cocoa powder and whisk until stiff peaks form.

Place 1 crepe on a cake stand or cake turner and spread evenly with the whipped cream mixture. Then, top with another crepe and spread that crepe evenly with apricot jam. Repeat, alternating crepe + cream, crepe + jam, and so on, until all the crepes are assembled into a stack.

Top with additional whipped cream and chocolate shavings, if desired, and serve. Store in an airtight container in the fridge for up to 3 days. If chilled, let the cake slices sit at room temperature before serving, about 15 minutes.

NOTE You see that the filling is very thin between the layers because, for me, it's the right balance of crepes and filling. If you prefer more filling, just increase the amount of whipped cream and jam to your liking.

Hands down, these cakes are one of my absolute favorite desserts. I don't know what it is that makes me so stupid about them because they are so simple, but just thinking about the gooey hot and liquid chocolate makes me weak. This recipe is so easy to make, and you will be rewarded big time for making it.

Chile Chocolate Lava Cakes

YIELD: **6** CAKES

1 tbsp (14 g) cold butter plus ¼ cup (23 g) unsweetened natural cocoa powder, for ramekins

9 oz (255 g) bar-style semisweet chocolate, finely chopped

¾ cup (170 g [1½ sticks]) unsalted butter

3 large eggs

3 large egg yolks

1 tsp vanilla extract

1 fresh Thai bird's eye chile, finely chopped, with or without seeds depending on your sensitivity to hot foods

½ cup (100 g) sugar

¼ cup (34 g) all-purpose flour, spooned and leveled

2 tbsp (11 g) unsweetened natural cocoa powder

¼ tsp salt

SERVING SUGGESTIONS

Powdered sugar, cocoa powder, ice cream, red pepper flakes, whipped cream or berries

Preheat the oven to 425°F (220°C). Butter the inside of six 1-cup (240-ml) ramekins and dust with cocoa powder so that the ramekins are completely covered on the bottom and sides. Place the ramekins in the freezer.

In a microwave-safe bowl, combine the chocolate and ¾ cup (170 g) of the butter and microwave on a medium setting, stirring every 20 seconds for 1 to 2 minutes, or until completely melted and well mixed. Set aside.

In a large bowl, whisk together the eggs, egg yolks, vanilla and chile just to combine. Then, in a medium bowl, whisk together the sugar, flour, cocoa powder and salt to combine. Add the flour mixture and the melted chocolate to the egg mixture and whisk just to combine. Do not overmix the batter at any step.

Remove the ramekins from the freezer and spoon the batter into the ramekins to fill them equally. Bake for 9 to 11 minutes, or until the edges are dry and set, and the center still looks wet.

Remove from the oven. Place a dessert plate on top of each ramekin. Then, flip over and invert each cake onto its plate. Please be cautious not to burn yourself as you do this; wearing oven mitts is strongly suggested.

Garnish the cakes with powdered sugar, cocoa powder, ice cream, red pepper flakes, whipped cream or fruit. Lava cakes are best eaten fresh when still warm. However, you can leave leftover cakes in their ramekins and store them, covered, at room temperature for up to 2 days. The center won't be liquid anymore, but the cold cakes are delicious as well. You can reheat them in the microwave.

NOTES: I'm used to eating hot food regularly, so I used the seeds of the Thai chile instead of discarding them. If you are sensitive to hot food and chiles, then remove the seeds. You could also add just ½ chile.

Be careful not to touch your face or eyes after cutting the chile and be sure to wash the cutting board, knife and your hands very well.

My mom used to bake angel food cake rolls a lot when I was a kid. I always loved the airy and cloudlike cake filled with whipped cream and served with loads of fresh berries. I thought my mother's recipe deserved a chocolaty twist and to be shared with you. It's just a lovely recipe, and it's easy to make. It's definitely the perfect cake for enjoying Sunday afternoons with your family.

Chocolate Angel Food Cake Roll

YIELD: 12 SERVINGS

CAKE

1⅔ cups (200 g) unpacked powdered sugar, plus 1 tbsp (8 g) for dusting, divided

¼ cup (34 g) all-purpose flour, spooned and leveled

¼ cup (21 g) unsweetened natural cocoa powder, spooned and leveled

6 large egg whites

1 tsp cream of tartar

Pinch of salt

WHIPPED CREAM

1 cup (240 ml) heavy whipping cream

1 tbsp (8 g) powdered sugar

1 tbsp (5 g) unsweetened natural cocoa powder

NOTE: If you desire, you can add strawberries, blackberries or raspberries to your filling. You will need about 1 cup (150 g) of fresh berries, but be careful that you don't overload the filling. Otherwise, it will be hard to roll up the cake again.

Make the cake: Preheat the oven to 325°F (160°C). Line a 9 x 13–inch (23 x 33–cm) baking pan with parchment paper and set aside.

In a medium bowl, sift together 1 cup (120 g) of the powdered sugar and the flour and cocoa powder and set aside.

In a large bowl, using an electric mixer fitted with a whisk attachment, whisk the egg whites, cream of tartar and salt on medium-high speed until soft peaks form, 3 to 5 minutes. Then, sift in the remaining ⅔ cup (80 g) of powdered sugar and continue to whisk on high speed until stiff peaks form and the meringue is stiff and glossy, about 5 minutes. Sift in the flour mixture in three batches, gently folding with a rubber spatula or wooden spoon until just combined. Do not overwork the meringue, or it will lose all its air and deflate.

Transfer the meringue batter to the prepared pan and spread evenly. Bake for 20 minutes.

Remove from the oven and let cool for 5 minutes. Then, use the parchment paper to lift the cake out of the pan. Lightly dust a clean, dry kitchen towel with the extra tablespoon (8 g) of powdered sugar, flip the cake roll onto the kitchen towel and gently peel off the parchment. Starting on a short side, roll up the cake in the kitchen towel and let cool completely on a wire rack, about 1 hour.

Make the whipped cream: In a large bowl, using an electric mixer fitted with a whisk attachment, whisk the cream on medium-high speed until soft peaks form, about 2 minutes. Then, add the powdered sugar and cocoa powder and whisk until stiff peaks form.

Slowly and carefully unroll the cake and spread the whipped cream mixture evenly on top. Tightly roll up the cake again (without using the towel) and refrigerate for 4 hours. Cut the cake roll into slices before serving. It will stay fresh in an airtight container in the refrigerator for up to 2 days.

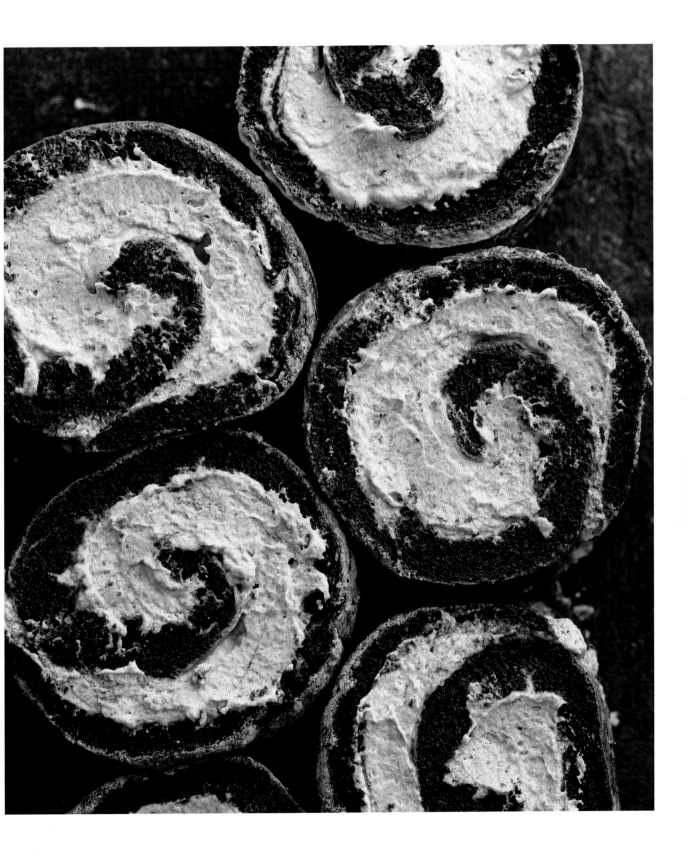

Sweet white chocolate cream cheese frosting is the perfect counterpart to this tangy lemon poppy seed sheet cake. It's like an explosion on your tongue. I know that this seems like an unusual pairing of flavors, but trust me, this cake just nails it. Even though this is not a chocolate cake recipe in a traditional sense, the white chocolate cream cheese frosting is just so good that it'll satisfy even the most addicted of chocoholics, and therefore well deserves its place in this chapter. It's a delicious and refreshing cake for every occasion.

Lemon Poppy Seed Sheet Cake with White Chocolate Cream Cheese Frosting

YIELD: **15** SERVINGS

CAKE

2 cups (270 g) all-purpose flour, spooned and leveled

2 tbsp (14 g) poppy seeds

2 tsp (8 g) baking powder

½ tsp salt

½ cup (113 g [1 stick]) unsalted butter, at room temperature

1¼ cups (250 g) sugar

2 large eggs

¼ cup (58 g) sour cream

2 tsp (10 ml) vanilla extract

1 tsp lemon zest

¼ cup (60 ml) milk

¼ cup (60 ml) fresh lemon juice

FROSTING

½ cup (113 g [1 stick]) unsalted butter, at room temperature

8 oz (227 g) cream cheese, softened

6 oz (170 g) bar-style white chocolate, melted and cooled

1 tsp vanilla extract

2 cups (240 g) unpacked powdered sugar

SERVING SUGGESTION

¼ cup (43 g) white chocolate shavings

Make the cake: Preheat the oven to 350°F (175°C). Line a 9 x 13-inch (23 x 33-cm) baking pan with parchment paper and set aside.

In a medium bowl, whisk together the flour, poppy seeds, baking powder and salt and set aside.

In a large bowl, using an electric mixer fitted with a whisk or paddle attachment, beat the butter and granulated sugar on medium-high speed until creamy and fluffy, 2 to 3 minutes. Add the eggs, one at a time, stirring just until combined, about 1 minute. Stir in the sour cream, vanilla and lemon zest and mix to incorporate, about 1 minute. Alternately add the flour mixture, milk and lemon juice, beginning and ending with the flour mixture, and whisk to combine, about 1 minute. The batter will be thick.

Transfer to the prepared baking pan. Bake for 25 to 30 minutes, or until a toothpick inserted into the center comes out clean.

Remove from the oven and let cool completely in the pan, 1 to 2 hours.

Make the frosting: In a large bowl, using an electric mixer fitted with a whisk or paddle attachment, beat the butter and cream cheese until fluffy and creamy, 2 to 3 minutes. Add the melted chocolate and vanilla and mix until well combined and smooth, about 2 minutes. Then, sift in the powdered sugar and whisk until combined, about 2 minutes.

Spread the frosting evenly on top of the cooled cake and let chill in the refrigerator for 2 hours. Cut the chilled cake and serve with white chocolate shavings on top, if desired. Store in an airtight container in the refrigerator for up to 3 days.

FESTIVE PIES
AND TARTS

Although pie season has its peak in fall when Thanksgiving is around the corner, I like to eat chocolate pies and tarts the whole year. For me, they don't have any season. At. All.

This wonderful chapter is packed with a wide variety of different pies and tarts every chocolate addict will love you for. From Baileys Dark Chocolate Pecan Chess Pie (page 115), to Rustic Chocolate–Grape Galette (page 121), to White Chocolate Macadamia Tart (page 125), to Dark Chocolate–Butterscotch Hand Pies (page 118), there is a chocolate recipe for everyone. Most of these pies and tarts are easy to make and require little preparation time. Enough talk; let's do it!

This recipe is actually Mario's invention. Thank God, I'm married to a genius. I used to make banana cream pie, but once Mario and I moved in together, he asked me whether I could make one for his birthday, but a chocolate banana cream pie instead. As one of the biggest chocolate addicts alive, I couldn't believe I hadn't thought of it before! It's just brilliant. If you love banana cream pie and chocolate, then baking this recipe should be a no-brainer for you.

Silky Banana Chocolate Cream Pie

YIELD: 16 SERVINGS

PIECRUST

1¼ cups (169 g) all-purpose flour, spooned and leveled, plus more for dusting

¼ tsp sugar

¼ tsp salt

½ cup (113 g [1 stick]) cold unsalted butter, chopped

4 to 6 tbsp (60 to 90 ml) cold water

FILLING

6 large egg yolks

¼ cup (32 g) cornstarch

2½ cups (600 ml) milk

¾ cup (150 g) sugar

¼ cup (59 g) mashed banana (about 1 medium banana)

7.5 oz (213 g) bar-style semisweet chocolate, very finely chopped

2 tsp (10 ml) vanilla extract

2 tbsp (28 g) unsalted butter

1 large very ripe banana, cut into ⅛ to ¼" (3- to 6-mm) slices

SERVING SUGGESTIONS

Whipped cream, fresh banana slices and chocolate shavings

Make the piecrust: In a food processor, combine the flour, sugar, salt and butter and pulse 4 or 5 times, or until pea-sized butter pieces are still visible. Add 1 tablespoon (15 ml) of the cold water at a time, pulsing one or two times after each addition. Stop adding water and pulsing when you notice that the dough comes together and starts to clump.

Without kneading the dough, transfer it to a sheet of plastic wrap and form into a 1- to 1½-inch (2.5- to 4-cm)-thick disk. Wrap tightly with plastic wrap and refrigerate for at least 2 hours or up to 2 days.

After chilling, on a lightly floured surface, roll out the dough into an 11-inch (28-cm) even circle and transfer to a 9-inch (23-cm) pie dish. Evenly press the dough into the bottom and against the sides of the pie dish and flute the edges. Freeze for 30 minutes.

While the crust is in the freezer, preheat the oven to 375°F (190°C).

Line the chilled piecrust with parchment paper and weight it down with pie weights, distributing them evenly and also pressing them lightly against the sides to prevent the sides from shrinking down too much.

Bake for 25 minutes. Then, remove from the oven and, being careful not to burn yourself, remove the pie weights along with the paper. Return the crust to the oven to bake for an additional 5 minutes, then remove from the oven and let cool for 30 minutes.

Make the filling: In a medium heatproof bowl, whisk together the egg yolks and cornstarch and set aside.

In a heavy-bottomed saucepan over medium heat, bring the milk and sugar to a simmer and cook for 2 minutes, stirring constantly.

Remove the saucepan from the heat and slowly spoon ½ cup (120 ml) of the hot milk into the egg yolk mixture, whisking as you go. Whisk constantly until the egg yolks and milk are well combined and smooth.

Then, slowly whisk the egg yolk mixture into the remaining hot milk mixture until well combined. Add the mashed banana and place the saucepan back over the heat. Cook the mixture until it thickens and looks like pudding, about 2 minutes, stirring constantly without stopping because it can burn quickly.

Remove from the heat and pour through a mesh strainer into a heatproof bowl, pressing the mixture through the strainer with a rubber spatula. Whisk in the chocolate and vanilla until combined. Cut the butter into a few pieces, add it to the mixture and whisk until it is melted and incorporated.

Place the banana slices in the baked and cooled piecrust, pour the filling on top of the banana slices and spread evenly. Cover the filling with plastic wrap and chill the pie in the fridge for at least 4 hours or preferably overnight.

Cut the chilled pie into slices and serve with whipped cream, fresh bananas and chocolate shavings, according to your taste. Store in an airtight container in the fridge for up to 3 days.

*See photo on page 6

NOTE: Please make sure that you cook the pudding until it's as thick as firm pudding; otherwise, the filling could end up being too soft and won't hold its shape after cutting.

I bet you'll hardly find two Mississippi mud pie recipes that are the same. It's one of those recipes for which gazillions of different versions exist. However, my favorite contains a crunchy base, a.k.a. chocolate cookie crust, followed by a fudgy chocolate brownie–like base, topped with supercreamy chocolate custard and garnished with loads of whipped cream. I know it also can be served with ice cream or can have just two layers, but for me, this is the best way to enjoy this special dessert. And I'm more than excited to share my favorite recipe for it with you!

The Ultimate Mississippi Chocolate Mud Pie

YIELD: 16 SERVINGS

PIECRUST

1½ cups (150 g) chocolate cookie crumbs

¼ cup (57 g [½ stick]) unsalted butter, melted

BROWNIE BASE

7.5 oz (213 g) bar-style semisweet chocolate, finely chopped

¾ cup (170 g [1½ sticks]) unsalted butter

¼ cup (60 ml) vegetable or canola oil

¾ cup (150 g) packed dark brown sugar

¾ cup (150 g) sugar

4 large eggs

2 tsp (10 ml) vanilla extract

1½ cups (203 g) all-purpose flour, spooned and leveled

½ cup (43 g) unsweetened natural cocoa powder, spooned and leveled

1 tsp salt

Make the piecrust: Preheat the oven to 350°F (175°C). Line a 9-inch (23-cm) springform pan with parchment paper by cutting out a circle plus a long strip for the sides. Set it aside.

In a large bowl, combine the cookie crumbs and melted butter and stir with a rubber spatula until evenly moist. Transfer to the prepared pan and press the crust into the bottom and a quarter of the way up the sides, using the base of a flat-bottomed cup. Bake for 10 minutes, then remove it from the oven and set it aside.

As the crust bakes, make the brownie filling: In a microwave-safe bowl, combine the chocolate and butter and microwave on a medium setting, stirring every 20 seconds, for about 2 minutes or until completely melted.

Transfer the chocolate mixture to a large bowl and add the oil, both sugars, eggs and vanilla and whisk just to combine, about 1 minute. Sift in the flour, cocoa powder and salt and whisk just until combined.

Transfer the batter to the prebaked crust and spread evenly. Covering the pie loosely with foil for the last 20 minutes, bake for 35 to 40 minutes, or until a toothpick inserted 1 inch (2.5 cm) away from the edge comes out clean with a few moist crumbs. Remove from the oven and let cool completely, about 2 hours.

(Continued)

The Ultimate Mississippi Chocolate Mud Pie (Continued)

4 large egg yolks

¼ cup (32 g) cornstarch

2 cups (480 ml) milk

½ cup (100 g) sugar

¼ cup (21 g) unsweetened natural cocoa powder, spooned and leveled

4.5 oz (128 g) bar-style semisweet chocolate, finely chopped

1 tsp vanilla extract

1 tbsp (14 g) unsalted butter

1 cup (240 ml) heavy whipping cream

2 tbsp (15 g) powdered sugar

Make the custard: In a medium heatproof bowl, whisk together the egg yolks and cornstarch and set aside.

In a heavy-bottomed saucepan over medium heat, bring the milk, sugar and cocoa powder to a simmer and cook for 2 minutes, stirring constantly.

Remove from the heat and spoon ½ cup (120 ml) of the hot milk mixture into the egg yolks, slowly whisking as you go. Whisk constantly until the egg yolks and milk are well combined and smooth.

Then, slowly whisk the egg yolk mixture into the milk mixture in the saucepan until well combined and place back over the heat. Cook the filling until it thickens and looks like pudding, about 2 minutes, stirring constantly because it can burn quickly.

Remove from the heat and pour through a mesh strainer into a heatproof bowl, pressing the filling through the strainer with a rubber spatula. Whisk in the chocolate and vanilla just until combined. Cut the butter into a few pieces, add it to the filling and whisk until it is melted and incorporated.

Transfer the custard to the chilled pie and spread evenly. Cover the custard with plastic wrap to prevent it from forming a skin on top. Chill the pie until the custard is completely set, at least 4 hours or overnight.

Make the whipped cream: In a large bowl, with an electric mixer fitted with a whisk attachment, whisk the cream on medium-high speed until soft peaks form, about 2 minutes. Then, add the powdered sugar and whisk until stiff peaks form, about 2 minutes.

Spoon the whipped cream on top of the pie and serve. Store in an airtight container in the fridge for up to 4 days.

This is my favorite Thanksgiving pie and everyone always raves about it when I serve it. I also serve some marshmallows and meringue with it so that everyone can decide on their own how they would like to enjoy their pie. The chocolate cinnamon roll piecrust is just mind-blowing with the sweet potato filling. Satisfaction guaranteed!

Sweet Potato Chocolate Cinnamon Roll Pie

YIELD: **16** SERVINGS

PIECRUST

2½ cups (338 g) all-purpose flour, spooned and leveled, plus more for dusting

¼ cup (21 g) unsweetened natural cocoa powder, spooned and leveled

2 tbsp (25 g) sugar

½ tsp salt

1 cup (226 g [2 sticks]) cold unsalted butter, chopped

8 to 10 tbsp (120 to 150 ml) cold water

CHOCOLATE CINNAMON SUGAR

¼ cup (50 g) sugar

2 tsp (5 g) ground cinnamon

2 tsp (4 g) unsweetened natural cocoa powder

2 tbsp (28 g) unsalted butter, at room temperature, to spread on the crust, divided

Make the piecrust: In a food processor, combine the flour, cocoa powder, sugar, salt and butter and pulse 4 or 5 times until larger butter pieces are still visible. Add 1 tablespoon (15 ml) of the cold water at a time, pulsing one or two times after each addition. Stop adding water and pulsing when you notice that the dough comes together and starts to clump.

Without kneading, divide the dough in half, transfer each half to a sheet of plastic wrap and form it into a 1- to 1½-inch (2.5- to 4-cm)-thick disk. Wrap each half tightly with plastic wrap and refrigerate for at least 2 hours or up to 2 days.

Make the chocolate cinnamon sugar: In a small bowl, combine the sugar, cinnamon and cocoa powder and set aside.

After it has chilled, on a lightly floured surface, roll out 1 piecrust into a square about ¼ inch (6 mm) thick. Spread 1 tablespoon (14 g) of the butter on top and sprinkle with half of the chocolate cinnamon sugar mixture. Starting on one side, roll the piecrust into a tight log and wrap tightly in plastic wrap. Repeat with the second piecrust. Refrigerate both rolled-up crusts for 1 hour.

Preheat the oven to 390°F (200°C).

Cut the chilled piecrusts into slices about ¼ inch (6 mm) thick and place in a 9-inch (23-cm) pie dish so that they touch one another and the bottom and the sides of the dish are completely covered. Press to seal the slices so that there is no space in between them. You will have leftover slices. Rewrap and place the leftover slices back in the fridge and freeze the pie dish for 10 minutes.

After the 10 minutes are up, bake the chilled piecrust for 10 minutes. Then, remove from the oven and set aside.

(Continued)

Sweet Potato Chocolate Cinnamon Roll Pie (Continued)

PIE FILLING

15 oz (425 g) canned or cooked sweet potato puree

14 oz (397 g) sweetened condensed milk

2 large eggs

2 tsp (10 ml) vanilla extract

1 tsp ground cinnamon

½ tsp salt

¼ tsp ground nutmeg

SERVING SUGGESTIONS

Marshmallows or meringue (page 134)

Lower the oven to 375°F (190°C).

Make the pie filling: In a large bowl, whisk together all the filling ingredients until combined. Pour into the prebaked crust and spread evenly. Bake for 15 to 20 minutes, or until the top is just set. Then, top the pie with the reserved piecrust slices and bake for an additional 25 minutes.

Remove from the oven and let cool completely, about 2 hours.

Chill the pie in the refrigerator for 4 hours before serving. Serve with toasted marshmallows or meringue, if desired. Refrigerate in an airtight container for up to 3 days (without any topping) or freeze for up to 1 month.

NOTE: If you'd like to serve your pie with fluffy meringue on top, you'll find a great recipe on page 134.

I'm in love with this recipe. Seriously. The Baileys taste combined with the dark chocolate is spectacular in this pie. Also, the textures are great: crunchy, creamy, flaky. Exactly how a perfect chocolate chess pie should be. The pecans are so flavorful and add so much depth to the pie. All in all, a wonderful recipe. If you don't want to use Baileys in this recipe, you can replace it 1:1 with milk. It will affect the taste, of course, but it's still delicious.

Baileys Dark Chocolate Pecan Chess Pie

YIELD: **16** SERVINGS

PIECRUST

1⅛ cups (152 g) all-purpose flour, spooned and leveled, plus more for dusting

¼ tsp sugar

¼ tsp salt

¼ cup (28 g) pecans, roughly chopped

½ cup (113 g) cold unsalted butter, chopped

4 to 6 tbsp (60 to 90 ml) cold water

FILLING

2 large eggs

1¼ cups (250 g) packed dark brown sugar

½ cup (43 g) unsweetened natural cocoa powder, spooned and leveled

½ cup (120 ml) Baileys Irish Cream

1 tsp vanilla extract

½ tsp salt

¼ cup (113 g [1 stick]) unsalted butter, melted

1½ cups (165 g) pecans, chopped

Make the piecrust: In a food processor, combine the flour, sugar, salt and pecans and pulse a few times. Then, add the butter and pulse 4 or 5 times, or until pea-sized butter pieces are still visible. Add 1 tablespoon (15 ml) of the cold water at a time, pulsing one or two times after each addition. Stop adding water and pulsing when you notice that the dough comes together and starts to clump.

Without kneading the dough, transfer it to a sheet of plastic wrap and form into a 1- to 1½-inch (2.5- to 4-cm)-thick disk. Wrap tightly with plastic wrap and refrigerate for at least 2 hours or up to 2 days.

After chilling, on a lightly floured surface, roll out the dough into an 11-inch (28-cm) even circle and transfer to a 9-inch (23-cm) pie dish. Evenly press the dough into the bottom and against the sides of the pie dish and flute the edges. Freeze the piecrust for 30 minutes.

While the crust is in the freezer, preheat the oven to 375°F (190°C).

Line the chilled piecrust with parchment paper and weight it down with pie weights, distributing the pie weights evenly and also pressing them lightly against the sides to prevent the sides from shrinking too much.

Bake for 10 minutes. Then, remove it from the oven and, taking care not to burn yourself, remove the pie weights along with the parchment paper, then set the piecrust aside.

Make the filling: In a large bowl, whisk together the eggs, brown sugar, cocoa powder, Baileys, vanilla and salt just to combine, about 1 minute. Stir in the melted butter to combine. Add the pecans and mix just to incorporate.

Pour the filling into the prebaked piecrust and bake the pie for 25 to 30 minutes, or until the top is set.

Remove it from the oven and let it cool completely, then transfer the pie to the fridge to chill for at least 4 hours.

Slice the pie before serving. Store in an airtight container in the fridge for up to 4 days or freeze for up to 1 month.

Not much can beat this pie! It's as if you wedded a chocolate custard pie to a blueberry pie, and they had a baby. As a heads-up, adding fresh blueberries will reduce the pie's shelf life because the berries will lose some water over time. So, bake up a fresh pie, top it with a mountain of ice cream, chocolate sauce and blueberries, and enjoy it.

Chocolate-Blueberry Custard Pie

YIELD: **16** SERVINGS

PIECRUST

1 cup (135 g) all-purpose flour, spooned and leveled, plus more for dusting

¼ cup (21 g) unsweetened natural cocoa powder, spooned and leveled

1 tbsp (13 g) sugar

¼ tsp salt

½ cup (113 g [1 stick]) cold unsalted butter, chopped

4 to 6 tbsp (60 to 90 ml) cold water

FILLING

2 large eggs

½ cup (100 g) sugar

2 tbsp (11 g) unsweetened natural cocoa powder

½ tsp ground cinnamon

¼ tsp salt

1¼ cups (300 ml) milk

1 tsp vanilla extract

2 level cups (400 g) fresh or frozen and thawed blueberries

SERVING SUGGESTIONS

Ice cream, whipped cream, chocolate sauce and fresh blueberries, if desired

Make the piecrust: In a food processor, combine the flour, cocoa powder, sugar, salt and butter and pulse 4 or 5 times, or until pea-sized butter pieces are still visible. Add 1 tablespoon (15 ml) of the cold water at a time, pulsing one or two times after each addition. Stop adding water and pulsing when you notice that the dough comes together and starts to clump.

Without kneading the dough, transfer it to a sheet of plastic wrap and form into a 1- to 1½-inch (2.5- to 4-cm)-thick disk. Wrap tightly with plastic wrap and refrigerate for at least 2 hours or up to 2 days.

After chilling, on a lightly floured surface, roll out the dough into an 11-inch (28-cm) even circle and transfer to a 9-inch (23-cm) pie dish. Evenly press the dough into the bottom and against the sides of the pie dish and flute the edges. Freeze for 30 minutes.

While the crust is in the freezer, preheat the oven to 375°F (190°C).

Line the chilled piecrust with parchment paper and weight it down with pie weights, distributing the pie weights evenly and also pressing them lightly against the sides to prevent the sides from shrinking down too much.

Bake the piecrust for 15 minutes. Then, remove it from the oven and, taking care not to burn yourself, remove the pie weights and the parchment paper, then set the piecrust aside.

Make the filling: In a large bowl, using an electric mixer fitted with a whisk or paddle attachment, beat the eggs on medium-low speed for 1 to 2 minutes. Add the sugar, cocoa powder, cinnamon and salt and mix just to combine, about 1 minute. Stir in the milk and vanilla until well incorporated.

Place the blueberries, in 1 layer, in the piecrust and pour the filling over them. Bake for 40 minutes.

Remove the pie from the oven and let it cool completely for 1 to 2 hours.

Transfer the pie to the fridge and chill for at least 4 hours before slicing. Store in an airtight container in the fridge for 1 day.

Dark Chocolate–Butterscotch Hand Pies

YIELD: 8 TO 10 HAND PIES

PIECRUST

1½ cups (203 g) all-purpose flour, spooned and leveled, plus more for dusting

⅓ cup (28 g) unsweetened Dutch-processed cocoa powder, spooned and leveled

2 tbsp (25 g) sugar

½ tsp baking powder

½ tsp salt

1 cup (226 g [2 sticks]) cold unsalted butter

½ cup (130 g) sour cream

1 large egg, lightly beaten

FILLING

½ cup (100 g) packed dark brown sugar

4 tsp (11 g) all-purpose flour

1 tbsp (14 g) unsalted butter, melted

1 tsp butterscotch extract

GLAZE

3 oz (85 g) bar-style semisweet chocolate, finely chopped

¼ cup (60 ml) heavy whipping cream

1 tsp butterscotch extract

Prepare the pie crust: In a large bowl, stir together the dry ingredients. Using a cheese grater, grate the butter into the flour mixture and work it in with a fork until it resembles a coarse meal and pea-sized butter flakes are still visible, being careful not to overwork. Using a rubber spatula, fold in the sour cream until incorporated, then gently knead a few times (don't overwork).

Transfer the dough to a lightly floured surface and roll it into an 8 x 10–inch (20 x 25–cm) rectangle and fold into thirds, business letter style. Rotate the dough 90 degrees and repeat the rolling and folding. Wrap the dough tightly with plastic wrap and place in the refrigerator to chill for at least 1 hour or up to 2 days.

Make the filling: In a medium bowl, stir together the brown sugar, flour, melted butter and butterscotch extract. Set aside.

Preheat the oven to 350°F (175°C). Line two baking sheets with parchment paper and set aside.

Roll out the chilled pie dough into a rectangle a little more than ⅛ inch (4 mm) thick. Cut into evenly sized rectangles so that you end up with an even number of rectangles, 16 to 20. Place 1 heaping tablespoon (15 g) of the filling in the center of 1 rectangle. Then, place another rectangle on top, seal the edges with the tines of a fork and cut 2 or 3 thin slits in the top that the steam can escape during baking. Repeat until you run out of dough and filling.

Brush the tops with the beaten egg and bake, one baking sheet at a time, for 22 to 24 minutes, or until the hand pies look puffed and flaky. Remove them from the oven and let the pies cool on the baking sheets to room temperature, 30 to 60 minutes.

Make the glaze: Place the chocolate in a heatproof bowl and set aside. In a microwave-safe cup, combine the cream and butterscotch extract and microwave on a medium setting for 1 to 2 minutes, or until it starts to simmer. Then, pour the cream mixture over the chocolate and let sit for 2 minutes. Stir the chocolate until completely combined, melted and smooth.

Drizzle the glaze over the hand pies and let dry for about 30 minutes. The hand pies are best eaten on the same or next day. Store in an airtight container at room temperature for up to 2 days.

*See photo on page 104.

I developed this tart for a friend of mine who loves everything with peanuts and chocolate (who doesn't?). She was completely blown away after the very first bite, and so was I. It's definitely a winner. This tart is very chocolaty and noticeably salty because of the salted peanuts. If you would like your tart to be more on the sweet side, consider using milk chocolate instead of semisweet and substitute unsalted peanuts.

Salted Peanut–Dark Chocolate Tart

YIELD: **16** SERVINGS

CRUST

1 cup (150 g) toasted salted peanuts, chopped

1 cup (135 g) all-purpose flour, spooned and leveled

1 tbsp (13 g) sugar

½ cup (113 g [1 stick]) cold unsalted butter, chopped

3 tbsp (45 ml) cold water

FILLING

12 oz (340 g) bar-style semisweet chocolate, finely chopped

1½ cups (360 ml) heavy whipping cream

¼ cup (57 g [½ stick]) unsalted butter

½ cup (75 g) toasted salted peanuts, chopped, plus more for serving, optional

Make the crust: In a food processor, combine the peanuts, flour and sugar and pulse a couple of times until the peanuts are ground. Add the butter and pulse 4 or 5 times, or until pea-sized butter pieces are still visible. Then, add 1 tablespoon (15 ml) of the cold water at a time, pulsing one or two times after each addition.

Transfer the mixture to a 9-inch (23-cm) pie dish with a removable bottom and evenly press the crumbs into the bottom and against the sides. Freeze the crust for 30 minutes.

While the crust is in the freezer, preheat the oven to 375°F (190°C).

Line the chilled crust with parchment paper and weight it down with pie weights, distributing the pie weights evenly and also pressing them lightly against the sides to prevent the sides from shrinking down too much.

Bake for 20 minutes with a piece of parchment paper underneath the pan to prevent liquid from dripping down to the bottom of your oven. Then, remove from the oven and, taking care not to burn yourself, remove the pie weights and parchment paper. Return the crust to the oven to bake for an additional 5 minutes, then remove from the oven and let cool for 30 minutes.

Make the filling: Place the chopped chocolate in a heatproof bowl and set aside. In a medium saucepan over medium-high heat, combine the cream and butter and bring to a boil. As soon as it reaches a boil, immediately remove the pan from the heat, pour the cream mixture over the chocolate and let stand for 2 minutes. Stir the chocolate until completely melted and smooth. Then, add the peanuts and stir to combine.

Immediately pour the filling into the crust and let it chill in the refrigerator for at least 4 hours or until it is set. Slice the chilled tart and serve with additional peanuts on top, if desired. Store in an airtight container in the refrigerator for up to 4 days.

*See photo on page 3.

Please tell me that you love grapes as much as I do. Great, but did you ever try to bake with them? Well, you should! Imagine a superflaky chocolate piecrust, topped with chopped milk chocolate bars and sweet grapes, mmm. I don't know about you, but I always loved that this galette tastes like chocolate-covered grapes. Well, those taste just like this but with the addition of a flaky chocolate piecrust. Best upgrade ever! I prefer to use high-quality milk chocolate bars, such as Ghirardelli, Lindt or Hershey's. You can also use chocolate chips, but be aware that they won't melt underneath the grapes as chocolate bars do.

Rustic Chocolate–Grape Galette

YIELD: **12** SERVINGS

FILLING

3 cups (450 g) red or green grapes, halved

¼ cup (50 g) sugar

1 tbsp (8 g) cornstarch

1 tsp vanilla extract

3 oz (85 g) bar-style milk chocolate, chopped

1 tbsp (14 g) unsalted butter

PIECRUST

1¼ cups (169 g) all-purpose flour, spooned and leveled, plus more for dusting

½ cup (43 g) unsweetened natural cocoa powder, spooned and leveled

¼ cup (50 g) sugar

½ tsp salt

½ cup (113 g [1 stick]) cold unsalted butter, chopped

4 to 6 tbsp (60 to 90 ml) cold water

Preheat the oven to 390°F (200°C). Line a baking sheet with parchment paper, then set aside.

Make the filling: In a large bowl, combine the grapes, sugar, cornstarch and vanilla and stir, then set aside.

Make the piecrust: In a food processor, combine the flour, cocoa powder, sugar, salt and butter and pulse 4 or 5 times, or until pea-sized butter pieces are still visible. Add 1 tablespoon (15 ml) of the cold water at a time, pulsing 1 to 2 times after each addition. Stop adding water and pulsing when you notice that the dough comes together and starts to clump.

On a lightly floured surface, roll out the dough into a ⅛- to ¼-inch (3- to 4-mm)-thick even circle and transfer to the prepared baking sheet.

Sprinkle the chopped chocolate over the piecrust but leave a 2- to 3-inch (5- to 7.5-cm) empty space around the edges. Then, using a slotted spoon, add the grapes, without any of their liquid, on top of the chopped chocolate. Fold the edges of the piecrust over the grapes and lightly press to seal them.

Cut the butter into a few pieces and dot on top of the grapes. Bake for 27 to 30 minutes, or until the piecrust is baked through and flaky.

Remove the galette from the oven and let it cool for about 30 minutes before slicing. A galette is best eaten the same day. Leftovers can be stored in the fridge for up to 1 day.

Greek yogurt provides a lot of calcium, and oatmeal contains a lot of fiber, vitamins and minerals. Among all baking recipes in this chocolate cookbook this tart is one of the healthier choices, but that doesn't mean it's boring or lacking in flavor. Far from it! The taste is amazing, and all those different layers and textures are just perfect in combination. So, grab a piece or two and enjoy it!

Chocolate Greek Yogurt Oatmeal-Crumble Tart

YIELD: 16 SERVINGS

CRUST

1 cup (100 g) old-fashioned rolled oats

½ cup (100 g) packed light brown sugar

¼ cup (34 g) all-purpose flour, spooned and leveled

2 tbsp (11 g) unsweetened natural cocoa powder

¼ tsp salt

6 tbsp (85 g) unsalted butter, melted

FILLING

3 large eggs

¾ cup (150 g) sugar

2 tsp (10 ml) vanilla extract

1½ cups (428 g) Greek yogurt

½ cup (68 g) all-purpose flour, spooned and leveled

¼ cup (21 g) unsweetened natural cocoa powder, spooned and leveled

TOPPING

½ cup (68 g) all-purpose flour, spooned and leveled

¼ cup (50 g) packed light brown sugar

¼ cup (25 g) old-fashioned rolled oats

Pinch of salt

¼ cup (57 g [½ stick]) cold unsalted butter

Preheat the oven to 350°F (175°C).

Make the crust: In a food processor, combine all the crust ingredients, except the butter, and pulse a few times until the oats are ground into smaller flakes. Add the melted butter and pulse a few times until the crumbs are evenly moist.

Transfer the crumbs to a 9-inch (23-cm) tart pan with a removable bottom and press the crumbs evenly into the bottom and the sides of the pan, then set aside.

Make the filling: In a large bowl, using an electric mixer fitted with a whisk attachment, whisk together the eggs, granulated sugar and vanilla until light, pale and fluffy, 2 to 3 minutes. Gently fold in the Greek yogurt just to combine. Then, gradually sift in the flour and cocoa powder and fold it in just to combine, until no lumps remain. Set aside.

Make the topping: In a medium bowl, stir together the flour, brown sugar, oats and salt. Cut the butter into the flour mixture and work it in with your fingers or a fork until it resembles coarse meal. Do not overwork; otherwise, it will become a paste instead of crumbs.

Place the filling in the crust and spread evenly. Evenly top the filling with the crumble topping. Place in the oven with a piece of parchment paper underneath the pan to catch any leaking liquid. Bake for 30 to 35 minutes, or until the filling is set and the topping golden brown.

Remove the tart from the oven and let it cool to room temperature for about 2 hours. Then, transfer to the refrigerator and let chill for 2 hours. Store in an airtight container in the refrigerator for up to 3 days.

This tart has the power to turn even non-white-chocolate lovers into fans of this recipe. The filling is so ridiculously creamy and tasty, and the macadamia graham cracker crust brings this tart to the next level. It's a simple and straightforward recipe that takes little time to prepare. So, a win-win situation.

White Chocolate Macadamia Tart

YIELD: **16** SERVINGS

CRUST

1½ cups (150 g) graham cracker crumbs

½ cup (75 g) roasted macadamia nuts, ground

1 tbsp (13 g) sugar

5 tbsp (71 g) unsalted butter, melted

FILLING

10.5 oz (298 g) bar-style white chocolate, finely chopped

1 cup (240 ml) heavy whipping cream

½ cup (120 ml) milk

2 large eggs, lightly beaten

1 tbsp (13 g) sugar

¼ tsp salt

SERVING SUGGESTIONS

Roasted macadamia nuts

Preheat the oven to 350°F (175°C).

Make the crust: In a large bowl, combine the graham cracker crumbs, ground macadamia nuts, sugar and melted butter and stir with a rubber spatula until the crumbs are evenly moist. Then, transfer the crumbs to a 9-inch (23-cm) pie dish with a removable bottom and press into the bottom and up the sides of the pan, using the base of a flat-bottomed cup.

Place in the oven with a piece of parchment paper underneath the pan to prevent liquid from dripping down to the bottom of your oven. Bake for 10 minutes, then remove the crust from the oven and set aside.

Make the filling: Place the chocolate in a heatproof bowl and set aside. In a small saucepan over medium-high heat, bring the cream and milk to a boil. As soon as it boils, immediately remove the pan from the heat and pour the cream mixture over the chocolate. Let stand for 2 minutes, then stir the chocolate until completely melted and smooth.

In a large bowl, whisk together the eggs, sugar and salt to combine. Then, add the chocolate mixture and whisk until well incorporated, about 1 minute.

Pour the filling into the crust and bake for 23 to 25 minutes (with the paper still underneath), or until the top is lightly browned.

Remove the tart from the oven and let cool completely, 1 to 2 hours. Transfer it to the refrigerator and let it chill for 4 hours. Slice the chilled tart and serve with additional macadamia nuts on top, if desired. Store in an airtight container in the refrigerator for up to 4 days.

NO-BAKE TREATS

Turn off the oven, but we're still "baking"! For me, no-bake chocolate treats are welcome all year round. It doesn't matter whether it's a hot summer day or a freezing cold winter day—they are always a great idea whenever you don't want to turn on the oven. There are gazillions of great no-bake chocolate recipes out there for every season and occasion. Get ready to dive into making chocolate ice cream (page 134), no-bake chocolate cheesecake (page 143), chocolate tiramisu (page 129), chocolate milk shakes (page 140), chocolate parfaits (page 130) and chocolate mousse (page 133).

I got a little creative to provide you with a broad mix of flavor combinations to spice things up a little. Think: avocado (page 134), mango (page 143), lavender (page 137) and Key lime (page 136), but also such classics as marshmallow (page 140), hazelnuts (page 130) and vanilla (page 133), all paired with all kinds of chocolate, of course. Every treat in this chapter requires a certain amount of chilling or freezing time, so make sure to factor that in when your chocolate cravings hit.

If I had to choose just five desserts to eat for the rest of my life, you can bet chocolate tiramisu would be one of them. Tiramisu is already a great dessert and a true Italian classic—adding chocolate makes it even better! Since I started making this version, no one ever requests regular tiramisu from me anymore! Aside from the addition of the cocoa powder to the mascarpone cream, this recipe is an authentic Italian tiramisu recipe, like you'd find in any good old Italian cookbook. Buon appetito!

Supercreamy Chocolate Tiramisu

YIELD: **12** SERVINGS

3 large egg yolks

1 cup (120 g) unpacked powdered sugar, sifted

¼ cup (21 g) unsweetened Dutch-processed cocoa powder, spooned and leveled, plus about 2 tbsp (21 g) for dusting

2¼ cups (500 g) cold mascarpone

27 to 36 Italian ladyfingers (hard ones)

½ to 1 cup (120 to 240 ml) cooled brewed espresso or strong coffee

In a large bowl, using an electric mixer fitted with a whisk attachment, beat the egg yolks, powdered sugar and cocoa powder on medium-high speed until creamy and the sugar is completely dissolved, 2 to 3 minutes. Add the mascarpone and mix until smooth and creamy, about 1 minute.

Quickly dip both sides of the ladyfingers into the coffee, 1 to 2 seconds per side, and arrange 9 to 12 ladyfingers on the bottom of a 9 x 7 x 3-inch (23 x 18 x 8-cm) or 8 x 8 x 3-inch (20 x 20 x 8-cm) casserole dish. The necessary number of ladyfingers will depend on the size of the ladyfingers as well as that of the casserole dish. The required amount of coffee depends on how long you dip the ladyfingers and how much they soak up. I don't recommend soaking the ladyfingers for too long; otherwise, the tiramisu will end up very watery.

Spread about one-third of the mascarpone cream on top of the ladyfingers. Repeat twice more, so that the tiramisu is assembled as follows from bottom to top: ladyfingers + cream, ladyfingers + cream, ladyfingers + cream.

Wrap the casserole dish tightly with plastic wrap so that no air or odors from the fridge can get inside the tiramisu. Refrigerate overnight for about 12 hours. Before serving, dust the top lightly with cocoa powder. Store in the fridge for up to 3 days.

NOTE: Please be aware that consuming raw eggs is at your own risk. Make sure to use only fresh eggs. If you have any concerns about eating raw eggs, then just skip the egg yolks and mix the mascarpone cheese with the sugar until creamy for 1 to 2 minutes. Without the egg yolks, you will have less cream. So, in this case, I recommend making just a two-layered tiramisu instead of three, or using a smaller casserole dish. You will also need fewer ladyfingers and less coffee.

Frozen chocolate parfait is something you will find in my freezer on any day throughout the whole year. Why? Whenever someone comes spontaneously to visit us, I always have something to serve and satisfy them. My mom is especially crazy about it, and if you asked her, she'd probably say that this is the best recipe in this cookbook. The chocolate parfait is so creamy and rich, and the layer with the toasted hazelnuts is something you could go bonkers over. Spoon alternately from both sides and combine both layers in your mouth. It's just heavenly.

Frozen Chocolate Toasted Hazelnuts Parfait

YIELD: **12** SERVINGS

10 large egg yolks (see note about consuming raw eggs, page 129)

1½ cups (300 g) superfine sugar

12 oz (340 g) bar-style 70% dark chocolate, melted

1½ cups (360 ml) heavy whipping cream

2 cups (300 g) blanched or roasted unsalted hazelnuts, roughly chopped

½ cup (148 g) chocolate spread, such as Nutella

Nonstick spray, for pan

NOTE: If you can't find roasted hazelnuts, you can use other roasted nuts instead or toast the hazelnuts yourself at 300°F (150°C) for 15 minutes, or until the skin cracks. Then, remove all the skins by placing the nuts in a clean, dry kitchen towel and rubbing and scrubbing them against one another.

In a large bowl, using an electric mixer fitted with a whisk attachment, beat the egg yolks and superfine sugar on medium-high speed until pale, creamy and the sugar is completely dissolved, 2 to 3 minutes. Add the melted chocolate and stir just until well combined, about 1 minute, then set aside.

In another large bowl, using a clean whisk attachment, whip the cream on medium-high speed until stiff peaks form, 2 to 3 minutes. Stir one-third of the whipped cream into the chocolate mixture until soft and smooth. Using a rubber spatula, gently fold the remaining two-thirds of the whipped cream into the chocolate.

In a medium bowl, combine the hazelnuts, chocolate spread and about 1 cup (240 ml) of the whipped chocolate mixture. Stir just to combine, about 1 minute, and set aside.

Line a 9 x 5–inch (23 x 13–cm) loaf pan with parchment paper with an overhang around the sides. Cut out the corners of the paper so that there is not too much overlapping of paper in the corners of the pan. Spray a bit of nonstick spray beneath the paper to stick it to the pan. Line the pan with plastic wrap on top of the parchment paper.

Evenly spread the remaining chocolate mixture in the pan and top evenly with the hazelnut mixture. Press it gently into the pan to even the top. Then, wrap tightly with plastic wrap and freeze overnight for about 12 hours.

Using the parchment, lift the frozen parfait out of the pan and remove the plastic wrap. Cut with a long, sharp knife into slices and then let stand at room temperature for 5 minutes before serving. Store in a freezer bag or container for up to 1 month.

White chocolate mousse is totally underrated in the world of chocolate mousse, don't you think? Luckily, I'm writing this recipe to correct that situation! I swear, this is my favorite chocolate mousse by far. Yes, I love dark chocolate mousse, but white chocolate is even better. Vanilla and white chocolate play so wonderfully together in this recipe. You can use either vanilla extract or the seeds of real Bourbon vanilla beans. It's terrific either way.

Airy Vanilla–White Chocolate Mousse

YIELD: **6** SERVINGS

1½ cups (360 ml) heavy whipping cream, divided

¼ cup (30 g) unpacked powdered sugar, sifted, divided

4 large egg yolks

7.5 oz (213 g) bar-style white chocolate, melted and cooled

2 tsp (10 ml) vanilla extract

SERVING SUGGESTIONS

Powdered vanilla bean, powdered sugar or white chocolate shavings

In a heavy-bottomed saucepan over low heat, combine ¾ cup (180 ml) of the cream, 2 tablespoons (15 g) of the powdered sugar and the egg yolks and whisk constantly until the mixture thickens and coats the back of a spoon, about 2 minutes. Don't allow to boil or simmer at any time.

Remove the pan from the heat and whisk in the melted chocolate and vanilla until smooth and incorporated. Chill the mixture in the fridge for about 1 hour.

In a large bowl, using an electric mixer fitted with a whisk attachment, whip the remaining ¾ cup (180 ml) of cream on medium-high speed until soft peaks form, about 2 minutes. Then, add the remaining 2 tablespoons (15 g) of powdered sugar and beat until soft peaks form.

Gently fold the whipped cream into the chocolate mixture. Do not overwork the cream, or your mousse won't be airy and light at all. Chill the mousse overnight in the fridge for 8 to 10 hours.

Spoon the chilled mousse into glasses or onto plates and top with powdered vanilla beans, powdered sugar or white chocolate shavings, if desired. Store in an airtight container in the fridge for up to 4 days.

NOTE: If you accidentally undercooked the custard, resulting in a mousse that is too soft to hold its shape, you may want to store it in the freezer and then remove it from the freezer 5 minutes before serving. This makes it more stable. Please be aware that, if frozen, the mousse will be creamy instead of fluffy and airy.

Maybe you're wondering, what the heck does the avocado do in baked Alaska? Homemade avocado-chocolate ice cream is actually mind-blowingly delicious. It's so creamy, and the avocado tastes great with the chocolate. If you don't have a thing for avocado, you can use your favorite chocolate ice cream for this amazing recipe instead.

Avocado-Chocolate Ice Cream Mini Baked Alaska with Chocolate Cookie Crust

YIELD: **12** SERVINGS

NO-CHURN AVOCADO-CHOCOLATE ICE CREAM

7 oz (200 g) sweetened condensed milk

3 oz (85 g) bar-style semisweet chocolate, melted

2 ripe avocados (12 oz [340 g] total), peeled, pitted and pureed

2 tbsp (11 g) unsweetened natural cocoa powder

1 tsp vanilla extract

¼ tsp salt

1½ cups (360 ml) heavy whipping cream

COOKIE CRUST

24 chocolate sandwich cookies, such as Oreos, including filling (266 g), crushed into fine crumbs

⅓ cup (75 g) unsalted butter, melted

MERINGUE

3 large egg whites

¾ cup (150 g) sugar

¼ tsp cream of tartar

Make the ice cream: In a large bowl, whisk together the condensed milk, melted chocolate, avocado puree, cocoa powder, vanilla and salt until combined and smooth, about 1 minute. Let chill in the fridge for about 20 minutes.

In a large bowl, using an electric mixer fitted with a whisk attachment, whip the cream until stiff peaks form, 1 to 2 minutes. Remove the chilled ice-cream base from the fridge and stir in one-quarter of the whipped cream until smooth and creamy. Carefully fold in the remaining three-quarters of the whipped cream just until combined. Do not overwork the whipped cream; otherwise it will lose too much air and deflate. Freeze the ice cream for about 4 hours, or until firm enough to scoop with an ice-cream scoop.

Make the crust: In a medium bowl, combine the cookie crumbs and filling with the melted butter and stir until the crumbs are evenly moist. Spoon the crumbs evenly into a 12-well muffin pan and press the crumbs into the bottom of each well. Freeze the crust for 1 hour. Remove the frozen cookie crust bottoms from the pan, place them on a large serving plate and freeze again for about 15 minutes. Then, scoop the ice cream on top of the frozen crust bottoms and freeze for 2 hours or overnight.

Make the meringue: Fill a saucepan about 2 inches (5 cm) deep with water and bring to a simmer over medium-low heat. Once the water is simmering, combine the egg whites, sugar and cream of tartar in a heatproof bowl and set it over the saucepan. The bowl should not touch the water. Whisk the egg whites constantly for 3 to 5 minutes, or until the sugar is completely dissolved. The meringue should be warm to the touch.

Remove the bowl from the heat and, using an electric mixer fitted with a whisk attachment, beat the egg whites on high speed until shiny, glossy and stiff peaks form, 5 to 7 minutes. Remove the prepared ice-cream cakes from the freezer and spoon or pipe the meringue on top of the cakes until they're completely covered, including the edges of the crust.

With a kitchen torch, lightly toast the meringue and serve immediately. Store in an airtight container in the freezer for up to 1 week.

These pie pops are not just insanely good, but also fun to eat. They're basically a no-bake Key lime pie with a chocolate crust, cut into pieces and covered with dark chocolate. Maybe you are a bit suspicious how Key lime and dark chocolate go together, but don't worry: Our beloved dark chocolate is so versatile and fits almost every food, so it's an out-of-this-world flavor experience—tangy, sweet, chocolaty. Just delicious!

No-Bake Dark Chocolate Key Lime Pie Pops

YIELD: 8 POPS

2½ cups (250 g) chocolate graham cracker crumbs, spooned and leveled

6 tbsp (85 g) unsalted butter, melted

12 oz (340 g) cream cheese, softened

14 oz (397 g) sweetened condensed milk

½ cup (120 ml) fresh Key lime juice

1 cup (240 ml) heavy whipping cream

12 oz (340 g) bar-style semisweet chocolate, finely chopped

2 tbsp (30 ml) vegetable or canola oil

NOTE: The chocolate is sufficient to cover the tops and sides of the pops. If you prefer to cover the bottom as well, you will need double the amount of chocolate. In this case, place the chocolate in a shallow bowl to dip all sides of the pops in chocolate.

In a medium bowl, stir together the graham cracker crumbs and melted butter until the crumbs are evenly moist. Then, transfer the crumbs to a parchment paper–lined 9-inch (23-cm) springform pan and press them into the bottom, using the base of a flat-bottomed cup, and about two-thirds up the sides of the pan. Freeze the crust for 15 minutes.

In a large bowl, using an electric mixer fitted with a whisk attachment, whip the cream cheese on medium-high speed until soft and creamy, about 2 minutes. Beat in the condensed milk to combine, about 1 minute. Then, add the lime juice and whip to incorporate, about 1 minute. Set aside.

In another large bowl, using a clean whisk attachment, whip the cream on medium-high speed until stiff peaks form, about 2 minutes. Gently fold the whipped cream into the Key lime cream until combined.

Remove the crust from the freezer. Fill with the Key lime filling, spreading evenly. Chill the pie in the fridge for 4 hours, or until the filling is set and the crust firm.

Take the chilled pie out of the fridge and cut into 8 slices (or 12, if you prefer smaller pops). Then, stick an ice pop stick straight through the crust into each slice. About 1½ inches (4 cm) of the stick should still extend from the back of the slice. You can precut little slits in the crust with a sharp, thin knife, if that is easier for you. Freeze the pops overnight.

In a microwave-safe bowl, combine the chopped chocolate and the oil and microwave on a medium setting, stirring every 20 seconds, for about 2 minutes, or until completely melted and mixed.

Remove the pops from the freezer and drizzle the chocolate on top of them to cover. Place back in the freezer to refreeze for about 1 hour.

Before serving, let the pops sit at room temperature for 5 to 10 minutes. Store in a freezer bag or container in the freezer for up to 1 month.

*See photo on page 126.

Ice-cream bars are the best for hot summer days, sitting in the backyard after a barbecue. These ice-cream bars are not overly sweet and so refreshing. I love the combination of white chocolate, blackberry and lavender. The lavender, which plays a key role in this recipe, has a very strong flavor. If you'd like to have a subtler, milder lavender flavor, you can reduce its quantity by half. It doesn't make a big difference whether you use dried or fresh lavender buds; I provided the recommended amount for both. However, it's important to use culinary-grade lavender and, if possible, organic. And the best part? This is a no-churn ice-cream recipe, so you don't need an ice-cream machine. Yay!

White Chocolate Blackberry Lavender Granola Ice-Cream Bars

YIELD: 14 TO 16 BARS

LAVENDER CREAM

2 tbsp (2 g) fresh or 1 tbsp (2 g) dried culinary-grade lavender buds

½ cup (120 ml) heavy whipping cream

NO-CHURN ICE CREAM

6 oz (170 g) sweetened condensed milk

4 oz (112 g) bar-style white chocolate, melted and cooled

2 tsp (10 ml) vanilla extract

½ tsp salt

1½ cups (360 g) heavy whipping cream

1 cup (150 g) fresh blackberries, roughly mashed

Nonstick spray, for pan

Make the lavender cream: Place the lavender buds in a small, heatproof bowl. In a small saucepan over medium-high heat, bring the cream to a simmer, then immediately remove the pan from the heat and pour the cream over the lavender. Cover with plastic wrap and chill in the fridge for 1 to 2 hours.

Make the ice cream: In a large bowl, whisk together the sweetened condensed milk, melted white chocolate, vanilla and salt until combined. Chill for 30 minutes in the fridge.

Sieve the lavender-infused cream and transfer to a large bowl, discarding all the lavender buds. Add the 1½ cups (360 g) of cream and, using an electric mixer fitted with a whisk attachment, whip until stiff peaks form.

Remove the chilled chocolate mixture from the fridge and add one-quarter of the whipped cream. Stir with a whisk until combined and smooth.

Use a rubber spatula to fold in the rest of the whipped cream just until nearly incorporated. Almost at the end of folding, add the mashed blackberries and fold a few times so that the ice-cream mixture looks marbled. The blackberries shouldn't be thoroughly combined with the ice cream. Do not overwork the ice cream; otherwise, the cream will flatten, which will result in hard rather than creamy ice-cream bars. Set the mixture aside.

Line a 9 x 13–inch (23 x 33–cm) pan with parchment paper. Cut out the corners of the parchment to fit it into the pan without having overlapping paper in the corners. Spray nonstick spray underneath the paper to stick it to the pan. Then, place a large piece of plastic wrap over the parchment. Transfer the ice cream to the prepared pan and spread evenly.

(Continued)

White Chocolate Blackberry Lavender Granola Ice-Cream Bars (Continued)

2 cups (180 g) plain or flavored granola of your choice

2 tbsp (28 g) unsalted butter, melted

12 oz (340 g) bar-style white chocolate, chopped

1 tbsp (15 ml) vegetable or canola oil

Make the granola: In a medium bowl, stir together the granola and melted butter until the granola is evenly moistened.

Transfer the granola to the pan, pressing it lightly and evenly on top of the ice cream. Wrap the pan tightly with plastic wrap and freeze for at least 8 hours or preferably overnight.

After chilling, use the plastic wrap to lift the ice cream out of the pan and cut into 14 to 16 bars. Using a warm, long knife makes it easier to cut the bars. Place the bars back in the freezer to refreeze for 1 hour.

Make the coating: In a microwave-safe bowl, combine the chocolate and oil and microwave on a medium setting, stirring every 20 seconds, until completely melted, 1 to 2 minutes.

Remove the bars from the freezer and drizzle the chocolate on top of the bars. Freeze again for 30 minutes, or until the chocolate has hardened.

Let the bars sit at room temperature 5 to 10 minutes before serving. Store in a freezer container in the freezer for up to 2 weeks.

If you have serious chocolate cravings that need to be satisfied in a blink of an eye, this superquick and easy recipe is your choice. This is my all-time favorite chocolate milk shake; it's so thick and creamy that you'll have trouble sucking it up through the straw. Exactly how a perfect milk shake should be, right? It also has chocolate curls in it, so you get some extra little pieces of chocolate to chew on. It's so simple to make, and you need just a handful of ingredients.

Extra-Thick and Creamy Marshmallow Chocolate Milk Shakes

YIELD: 2 MILK SHAKES

1 pint (475 ml) chocolate ice cream

½ cup (120 ml) milk

1 cup (100 g) marshmallow fluff

1 tsp vanilla extract

¼ cup (43 g) semisweet chocolate curls

SERVING SUGGESTIONS

Chocolate fudge sauce, toasted marshmallows and salty pretzels

In a blender or food processor, combine the ice cream, milk, marshmallow fluff and vanilla and blend until smooth, creamy and evenly mixed. Then, add the chocolate curls and stir just until they are evenly distributed.

Transfer the milk shake to two tall glasses and top with chocolate fudge sauce, toasted marshmallows and salty pretzels, if desired.

NOTE: These milk shakes are very thick. You can add more milk to create a thinner milk shake, if preferred.

This no-bake white chocolate cheesecake will give you a summery feeling. Tropical fruits fit white chocolate so dang well! Although the mango topping is irresistibly delicious, you can replace it with any other fruit you love, such as other tropical fruits or berries. Not in the mood for fruits at all? No problem! Just skip the topping altogether and enjoy this supercreamy no-bake white chocolate cheesecake on its own.

No-Bake White Chocolate–Mango Cheesecake

YIELD: **16** SERVINGS

2 cups (200 g) chocolate graham cracker crumbs

6 tbsp (85 g) unsalted butter, melted

1½ lbs (680 g) cream cheese, softened

1½ cups (300 g) sugar

12 oz (340 g) bar-style white chocolate, melted and cooled

2 tsp (10 ml) vanilla extract

1 cup (240 ml) heavy whipping cream

½ cup (120 ml) hot water

1 tbsp (9 g) powdered gelatin

1 cup (250 g) mango puree (from about 1 mango)

In a medium bowl, combine the chocolate graham cracker crumbs and the melted butter and stir until the crumbs are evenly moist. Then, transfer the crumbs to a parchment paper–lined 9-inch (23-cm) springform pan, pressing them into the bottom, using the base of a flat-bottomed cup, and about halfway up the sides of the pan. Freeze the crust for 15 minutes.

In a large bowl, using an electric mixer fitted with a whisk attachment, whip the cream cheese and sugar on medium-high speed until soft, about 2 minutes. Then, add the melted chocolate and vanilla and whip until creamy and incorporated, about 2 minutes. Add the cream and mix until soft peaks form, for 2 to 3 minutes.

Remove the crust from the freezer and add the filling, evenly spreading it over the crust. Cover the top with plastic wrap, then chill the cheesecake for about 4 hours in the fridge, or until set.

In a heatproof bowl, combine the hot water and gelatin powder and stir until the powder is dissolved and combined with the water, about 1 minute. Then, add the mango puree and whisk to combine.

Remove the plastic wrap from the cheesecake. Spoon the mango mixture on top and spread evenly. Refrigerate the cheesecake overnight, about 8 hours.

Slice the cheesecake before serving. Store in an airtight container in the fridge for up to 2 days.

NOTE: If you can't find chocolate graham crackers, you can also use chocolate wafers or chocolate cookies. Keep in mind that the texture of the crust will differ slightly in this case.

SWEET CANDIES

Welcome to Chocolate Candy Land! With this chapter, all your inner-child's dreams can come true. It's full of all the good stuff we've been loving since we were little kids, but in the chocolate version! From chocolate toffee (page 151), to chocolate taffy (page 159), to chocolate marshmallows (page 147), to chocolate pralines (page 155), to chocolate truffles (page 148) to chocolate fudge (page 152), here is everything that your chocolate candy–feasting heart could ever desire.

Some of these recipes are very simple to make; some require muscle power; others, a bit of patience. I guarantee that you will have lots of fun re-creating the recipes in this chapter. So, although it's not the easiest chapter in this book, it's one of the most exciting, for sure. You'll love reveling in nostalgia and remembering some beautiful childhood memories, perhaps while creating new ones with your own kiddos. That makes this chapter so special and unique. I chose recipes that are easy to follow, and I've provided you with all my knowledge, tips and tricks to make sure that even the more challenging recipes come together as flawlessly as possible.

These marshmallows are beyond pillowy and HUGE. They taste like you are eating hot chocolate in the form of a cloud. Making marshmallows is an easy but long process. Be patient and you will be rewarded with the best-ever chocolate pistachio marshmallows.

Pillowy Chocolate-Pistachio Marshmallows

YIELD: 16 JUMBO MARSHMALLOWS

MARSHMALLOWS

7 tsp (21 g) powdered gelatin

1 cup (240 ml) water, divided

2 cups (400 g) sugar

½ cup (120 ml) light corn syrup

¼ tsp salt

¼ cup (21 g) unsweetened natural cocoa powder, spooned and leveled

½ cup (75 g) shelled pistachios, chopped

Nonstick spray or oil, for pan, spatula and hands

½ cup (60 g) unpacked powdered sugar

¼ cup (21 g) unsweetened natural cocoa powder, spooned and leveled

¼ cup (32 g) cornstarch

NOTES: Please resist the urge to stir the cooking sugar syrup. Otherwise, it won't fluff up when it is mixed.

Also, a candy thermometer is crucial for the success of this recipe.

Make the marshmallows: In a large bowl, using an electric mixer fitted with a whisk attachment, whisk together the gelatin and ½ cup (120 ml) of the water. Set aside until the sugar syrup has finished cooking, during which time the gelatin will have "bloomed."

In a large saucepan over medium-low heat, combine the remaining ½ cup (120 ml) of water, granulated sugar, corn syrup and salt and bring to a low simmer without stirring. Cook the mixture without stirring at any time until it reaches 240°F (116°C), about 15 minutes. Use a candy thermometer to check the temperature.

Meanwhile, prepare the pan: Lightly grease a 9-inch (23-cm) square baking pan. Then, in a small bowl, combine the powdered sugar, cocoa powder and cornstarch and generously sift about one-quarter of the mixture into the pan to cover the bottom and the sides completely. Also, grease a rubber spatula and set aside.

Once the syrup has reached the required temperature, immediately remove it from the heat and pour the mixture into the bowl of bloomed gelatin. Start whisking the mixture at low speed and steadily increase the speed to high within the first 30 seconds. Whisk until very thick, multiplied several times in size and still warm to touch; this takes 6 to 10 minutes. Then add the cocoa and pistachios and whisk just until incorporated. Using the prepared spatula, quickly transfer the marshmallow mixture to the prepared pan. Then, oil your hands and gently even the top by pressing the marshmallow mixture into the pan. Dust generously with about one-quarter of the powdered sugar mixture. Let the marshmallows dry for at least 4 hours or overnight.

Dust a clean surface with a little of the powdered sugar mixture and invert the pan onto it. Lightly tap the pan to release the marshmallows from the pan. If the marshmallows don't come out on their own, run a knife around the edges of the pan. Dust the top of the marshmallows with one-quarter of powdered sugar mixture and let them dry for another 4 hours.

Dust a long, sharp knife with some of the remaining powdered sugar mixture and cut into 16 jumbo marshmallows. They will be about 2 x 2 x 2 inches (5 x 5 x 5 cm). After each cut, dust the knife again. Then, toss the marshmallows in the remaining powdered sugar mixture and enjoy. Store the marshmallows in an airtight container at room temperature for up to 1 week.

You need just five ingredients to make these tasty truffles. But the fact that these chocolate truffles are supereasy and quick to make isn't even the best thing about this wonderful recipe. The texture and the taste are what will make you go crazy! The dark chocolate literally melts in your mouth, and then you get to chew on the almond pieces. It's just pure joy to eat them.

Dark Chocolate–Almond Truffles

YIELD: **24** TRUFFLES

½ cup (113 g [1 stick]) unsalted butter, at room temperature

9 oz (255 g) bar-style semisweet chocolate, melted and cooled

2 tbsp (30 ml) heavy whipping cream

½ tsp almond extract

½ cup (70 g) blanched almonds, finely chopped

In a large bowl, using an electric mixer fitted with a whisk or paddle attachment, beat the butter until light and fluffy, about 2 minutes. Then, add the melted chocolate and whisk to incorporate, about 1 minute. Add the cream and almond extract and stir to combine, about 1 minute. Then, stir in the almonds until fully incorporated, about 1 minute.

Chill the mixture for about 1 hour, or until firm enough to scoop and roll into balls. I prefer my truffles to be about 2 tablespoons (20 g) in size, but you can adjust the size to your liking. Use an ice-cream or cookie scoop, then very quickly roll the scoops with the palm of your hands into smooth balls. If you don't mind that the bottom of the truffles are flat, you can just scoop them and skip the rolling.

Chill the truffles for 1 hour before serving. Store in an airtight container in the fridge for up to 1 week.

NOTE: I prefer using blanched almonds because they have no skin. But you can use any kind of almonds, whichever you like the most.

I can tell you that the apple cider vinegar in this toffee makes the taste so out-of-the-world fantastic. The combination of all the flavors is a match made in heaven. The texture of this chocolate-covered toffee is amazing as well. Expect a supercrunchy and delicious toffee base topped with milk chocolate and macadamia nuts. If this doesn't sound irresistible to you, I don't know what does. You can also top the toffee with white or dark chocolate, of course. I recommend using high-quality chocolate bars from a brand you love, to have the best toffee possible.

Apple Cider Chocolate Macadamia Toffee

YIELD: **24** SERVINGS

1 cup (226 g [2 sticks]) unsalted butter

1 cup (200 g) sugar

¼ cup (60 ml) apple cider vinegar

½ tsp salt

1 tsp vanilla extract

6 oz (170 g) bar-style milk chocolate

1 cup (150 g) roasted macadamia nuts, roughly chopped

Line a 9-inch (23-cm) square baking pan with parchment paper and set aside.

In a heavy-bottomed saucepan over medium-low heat, combine the butter, sugar, vinegar and salt and bring the mixture to a boil. Stir until the sugar is dissolved, then cook the mixture until it reaches 290°F (143°C). This takes about 10 minutes. Use a candy thermometer to check the temperature. Turn off the heat and stir in the vanilla.

Pour the mixture into the prepared baking pan and let sit for 10 minutes. Place the chocolate bars on top and let sit for 5 minutes. When the chocolate is melted, spread it evenly with the back of a spoon and evenly scatter the macadamia nuts on top. Let the toffee cool at room temperature until completely hardened, about 2 hours.

Using the parchment paper, lift the toffee out of the pan and break it into pieces. Store the toffee at room temperature for up to 2 weeks.

NOTE: You can use either unsalted or salted and also roasted or raw macadamia nuts, according to your preference. I like the taste of unsalted roasted macadamia nuts the most.

Mario before I made this recipe: "I don't think that the honey-roasted cashews are a good idea to add to the chocolate fudge". Mario after he tried the fudge: "Okay, I'm sorry that I even dared to question this. Those honey-roasted cashews in the chocolate fudge are a game-changer. Never, ever make chocolate fudge without the cashews anymore." Well, there is nothing more to say about this recipe. That pretty much sums it up.

Honey-Roasted Salted Cashew Chocolate Fudge

YIELD: 81 PIECES

Unsalted butter, for pan

2 cups (300 g) whole honey-roasted cashews

3 cups (600 g) sugar

⅔ cup (56 g) unsweetened natural cocoa powder, spooned and leveled

1½ cups (360 ml) milk

⅛ tsp salt

¼ cup (57 g [½ stick]) unsalted butter

1 tsp vanilla extract

Line a 9-inch (23-cm) square baking pan with parchment paper and lightly butter the paper. Then, distribute the cashews evenly on the bottom of the pan and set aside.

In a medium saucepan over medium heat, combine the sugar, cocoa, milk and salt and stir constantly with a wooden spoon (do not use a metal spoon; otherwise, the fudge will take longer to reach the required temperature and the spoon will get very hot) until it starts to reach a strong boil. This takes 10 to 15 minutes. Then, lower the heat to low, stop stirring and continue to cook until the mixture reaches 234°F (112°C). Use a candy thermometer to check the temperature.

Remove from the heat, place the butter and vanilla on top of the fudge and let it cool to 110°F (43°C) without stirring, again checking the temperature with a candy thermometer. Then, stir with a wooden spoon until the fudge starts to lose its sheen, 5 to 7 minutes.

Quickly pour the fudge on top of the cashews and let cool at room temperature overnight, 10 to 12 hours.

Using the parchment paper, lift the fudge out of the pan and cut it into 81 pieces. Store at room temperature for up to 2 weeks.

NOTE: It's crucial to use a candy thermometer for making fudge. Otherwise, it's likely that the fudge will be undercooked and won't set.

This easy-to-follow recipe takes the intimidation factor out of making pralines, so you can just focus on wowing your friends and family with these candies. The combination of a dark chocolate shell filled with cooked orange ginger syrup and white chocolate orange cream is so sophisticated and unique. Don't stint on the quality of the chocolate. I highly recommend using Lindt or Ghirardelli.

Dark and White Chocolate Orange-Ginger Pralines

YIELD: **20** PRALINES

1 cup (240 ml) fresh orange juice

¾ cup (150 g) plus 2 tbsp (25 g) sugar, divided

6 oz (170 g) bar-style semisweet chocolate, melted

2 tbsp (28 g) unsalted butter, at room temperature

2 oz (56 g) bar-style white chocolate, melted and cooled

2 tbsp (30 ml) heavy whipping cream

NOTES: If you want to top your pralines with candied orange pieces as I did, then see the recipe on page 70. You will need just one-quarter of the recipe for the candied oranges.

The required amount of chocolate, orange syrup and chocolate cream for each praline will depend on the size of your mold. My pralines are about 1⅓ inches (3.6 cm) wide and ⅔ inch (1.6 cm) high.

In a medium saucepan over medium-high heat, bring the orange juice and ¾ cup (150 g) of the sugar to a boil. Cook until the mixture thickens and is reduced by half, about 10 minutes. The consistency should be almost like that of syrup. Remove from the heat and let cool for 1 hour. It will thicken as it cools.

Spoon about ½ to 1 teaspoon of the melted semisweet chocolate into each divot of a silicone chocolate praline mold or the non-hole side of a silicone cake pop mold. Then, swirl the mold in a circle to completely cover the inside of all the divots with chocolate and gently but quickly flip the mold upside down and let the excess chocolate drip off back into the bowl. Place the mold, open side down, on a wire rack to let the chocolate dry and harden completely for about 1 hour. Store the remaining chocolate in a warm place so that it stays liquid or reheat if necessary. After the chocolate shells have hardened, carefully use a sharp knife to cut off any chocolate that's spilled outside the divots, if necessary.

Spoon ½ teaspoon of the cooled orange syrup into each hardened chocolate shell. Set the remaining orange syrup aside.

In a small bowl, using an electric mixer fitted with a whisk attachment, beat the butter and the remaining 2 tablespoons (25 g) of sugar until the sugar is dissolved and the mixture is creamy, 1 to 2 minutes. Then, add the melted white chocolate along with the remaining orange syrup and whisk until creamy and fully combined, 1 to 2 minutes. Stir in the cream and whisk until creamy and combined, 1 to 2 minutes.

Spoon the cream mixture into the chocolate shells until almost full. You will need about ½ tablespoon (7 ml) per praline. Then, spoon the remaining semisweet chocolate on top and even out with the edge of a large offset spatula. Let the pralines dry at room temperature for 1 hour. Then, place in the fridge and let chill for 2 hours.

Invert the silicone mold and quickly but gently push the pralines out of the mold. Top with candied orange pieces, if desired, and serve. Store in the fridge for up to 2 weeks.

Picture coffee-infused mascarpone truffles dipped in melted chocolate and covered with cocoa powder. Imagine your thoughts are racing about whether you have all the ingredients at home or where the heck you get them as fast as possible, and your excitement level is rapidly rising because you're already picturing tasting these yummy little chocolate treats. Trust me; the excitement level will further increase once you put the first truffle in your mouth. They're addictive!

Chocolate-Covered Tiramisu Truffles

YIELD: **36** TRUFFLES

2⅓ cups (204 g) hard Italian-style ladyfinger crumbs, spooned and leveled

1 tbsp (13 g) sugar

½ cup (111 g) mascarpone

2 to 3 tbsp (30 to 45 ml) cold, strongly brewed coffee, such as espresso

12 oz (340 g) bar-style semisweet chocolate, melted and cooled

2 tbsp (11 g) unsweetened Dutch-processed cocoa powder

In a large bowl, combine the ladyfinger crumbs and sugar. Add the mascarpone and mix, with an electric mixer fitted with the whisk attachment or by hand with a whisk, just to combine, about 1 minute. Then, add 1 tablespoon (15 ml) of the coffee at a time and stir to combine. Stop adding coffee when the mixture has the texture of raw cookie dough. Cover the bowl with plastic wrap and refrigerate for 1 hour.

Spoon 1 tablespoon (about 10 g) of the mixture into balls, or make them whatever size you prefer, and roll into smooth balls with the palm of your hands. Freeze for 15 minutes.

In the meantime, line a cookie sheet with parchment paper and set aside. Remove just 6 balls at a time and dip each of them into the melted chocolate. Place them, just enough apart that they don't touch each other and don't stick together, on a parchment paper–lined sheet and let them dry. Repeat until all the truffles are covered with chocolate. Refrigerate for 1 hour.

Dust the chilled truffles with cocoa powder and enjoy. Store in an airtight container in the refrigerator for up to 3 days.

Chocolate taffy has always been a favorite candy of mine, and the slight rum aroma is like the cherry on top. It's chewy and oh so good. Being successful in making taffy is all about time management. It's crucial that you start pulling, twisting and folding the taffy as soon as you can handle it, wearing kitchen gloves, which are an absolute necessity, by the way. Do not let the cooked taffy get too cold and stiff. Otherwise, you won't be able to work with it long enough to give it that characteristic taffy consistency. Be sure to butter your gloves, to make sure the taffy doesn't stick to them. Making this taffy is such a fun and unique experience, but it also requires some muscle power and patience. You will see, the effort is absolutely worth it.

Beyond Chewy Rum Chocolate Taffy

YIELD: **60** TAFFIES

About 2 tbsp (28 g) unsalted butter, at room temperature, for parchment, gloves and scissors

1½ cups (300 g) sugar

⅓ cup (28 g) unsweetened natural cocoa powder, spooned, leveled and sifted

½ tsp salt

¾ cup (180 ml) light corn syrup

1 tbsp (14 g) unsalted butter

1 tsp apple cider vinegar

1 tsp rum extract

Line a baking sheet with parchment paper and lightly butter the parchment. Set aside.

In a heavy-bottomed saucepan over medium heat, combine the sugar, cocoa powder, salt, corn syrup, butter and apple cider vinegar and bring to a boil. Stir until the sugar is dissolved, about 5 minutes. Then, lower the temperature to low and continue to cook until the mixture reaches 255°F (124°C) without stirring. Use a candy thermometer to check the temperature.

Turn off the heat and stir in the rum extract. Then, pour the mixture onto the prepared baking sheet and let cool until it is cool enough to handle, about 15 minutes.

Put on kitchen gloves and liberally butter them. Fold the warm taffy in half on the sheet a couple of times. Then, pick it up and start to pull, twist and fold back the taffy, buttering your gloves regularly. Continue until the taffy is lighter in color and has lost its sheen. This process takes 10 to 15 minutes. The taffy is ready to cut when it gets stiff and it becomes difficult to pull.

Pull and shape the taffy into a long log about 1 inch (2.5 cm) thick. Liberally butter a pair of kitchen scissors and cut the taffy into 1-inch (2.5-cm) pieces. Wrap each piece in waxed paper. Store at room temperature for up to 2 weeks.

You will think you are on a trip in the Caribbean when you bite into one of these candies. The soft and creamy papaya filling in the center of the white chocolate shell is just brilliant. I love to store them in the fridge on hot summer days to always have a snack to cool myself down. If you don't like papaya, or if it isn't available near you, you can try to make this recipe with any other pureed tropical fruit, such as kiwi, mango or passion fruit, to name just a few. I'm fond of this recipe because it's easy and so delicious!

White Chocolate Papaya Cups

YIELD: **12 CUPS**

4 large egg yolks

1 tbsp (8 g) cornstarch

½ cup (125 g) papaya pulp

¼ cup (50 g) sugar

1 tbsp (15 ml) fresh lemon juice

2 tbsp (28 g) cold unsalted butter, cut into a few pieces

18 oz (510 g) bar-style white chocolate, chopped

NOTE: You can also use smaller liner cups, if preferred. In this case, you will end up with 25 to 30 chocolate cups.

In a small bowl, whisk together the egg yolks and cornstarch just until combined, then set aside.

In a small saucepan over medium heat, combine the papaya pulp, sugar and lemon juice and heat until it reaches a simmer, 2 to 3 minutes. Lower the heat to low. Remove about ¼ cup (60 ml) of the hot fruit pulp and whisk into the egg yolks to temper them. Pour the tempered egg yolks into the saucepan, and continue to cook, whisking constantly, for about 2 minutes, or until the fruit mixture thickens and coats the back of a spoon.

Remove the saucepan from the heat and stir in the butter. Let the mixture cool to room temperature, about 1 hour.

Place two-thirds of the white chocolate in a microwave-safe bowl and microwave on a medium setting, stirring every 20 seconds, until melted, about 2 minutes. Remove the chocolate from the microwave and add the remaining white chocolate, stirring occasionally until it's completely melted.

Spoon three-quarters of the melted chocolate into 12 thick paper or silicone cupcake liners (silicone is easier to work with). Using a small, clean pastry brush, brush the chocolate until up to the edges of the liners. Let sit for about 5 minutes, or until the chocolate starts to set around the edges.

Invert the liners and let the excess chocolate drip back into the bowl, then place them upside down on a parchment paper–lined baking sheet. Let dry at room temperature for 1 hour. Store the leftover chocolate in a warm place to keep it liquid.

Spoon the pulp into the chocolate cups and spoon the remaining white chocolate on top. Let the cups dry at room temperature for 1 hour.

Remove the cups from the liners and serve. Store in the fridge for up to 4 days.

IMPRESSIVE BREADS AND PASTRIES

This is, hands down, one of my favorite chapters in this book. It is such a beautiful collection of different recipes that require a bit of patience and love to make them an unforgettable treat. They include ultraflaky chocolate croissants (page 173) and braided chocolate brioche bread (page 178)—these delicate pastries can be tricky to make, but I promise you that they're worth it! And I'll be here to walk you through each step, so you'll be breakfasting or brunching on them in no time.

On the next pages, you will find everything your chocolate-loving heart could crave. Think: chocolate donuts (page 167) for breakfast. Yes. Think: chocolate brioche Danishes (page 181) for your Saturday brunch. Oh, yes. Think: chocolate monkey bread (page 165) for fun game nights with friends. Double yes. Think: white chocolate cream puffs (page 187) for family retreats. Yes, yes and yes.

After baking your way through this chapter, you'll be a master home baker and no baking recipe ever will make you sweat. So, let's jump in and make your future breakfasts and brunches unforgettable events.

A note about baking with yeast: When baking with yeast, it's very easy to tell whether your yeast is already dead or still active. Whenever you bake one of the recipes that starts with combining yeast with other ingredients, such as warm milk and sugar, and you need to let it stand for 5 to 10 minutes, it really needs to get foamy on the surface within the first 10 minutes. If nothing happens in this time and the mixture still looks the same as in the beginning, it's almost certain that your baked good won't rise very much or at all during the baking process. It's better to stop here and start again using fresh yeast that is still active.

This recipe will fulfill your wildest triple-chocolate dreams. The dough is made with cocoa powder, then the knots are filled with chopped chocolate and the dipping sauce is like pure melted chocolate. It's easier than you might think to re-create the characteristic taste and texture of pretzels. All you need to make the magic happen is ½ cup (120 g) of baking soda—yes, that much! You can shape the dough in every way you want, but I'm obsessed with the knots shape lately, so I had to make knots. This recipe is just perfect for game nights . . . and for every other occasion as well, of course.

Cinnamon Sugar Dark Chocolate Pretzel Knots with Chocolate Dipping Sauce

YIELD: **10** PRETZEL KNOTS

PRETZEL KNOTS

10 cups (2.4 L) plus 1½ cups (360 ml) water, divided

1 tbsp (13 g) sugar

2¼ tsp (7 g) active dry yeast

¼ cup (57 g [½ stick]) unsalted butter, melted

1 tsp salt

1 tbsp (5 g) unsweetened natural cocoa powder

3¼ to 3½ cups (439 to 473 g) all-purpose flour, spooned and leveled, plus more for dusting

Nonstick spray, for bowl

6 oz (170 g) bar-style semisweet chocolate, chopped

½ cup (120 g) baking soda

1 large egg, lightly beaten

Make the pretzel knots: Preheat the oven to 200°F (100°C). Line two baking sheets with parchment paper and set aside.

In a large bowl, using an electric mixer fitted with a whisk attachment, stir together 1½ cups (360 ml) of the water, sugar and yeast to combine. Then, let sit for 5 to 10 minutes, or until the surface starts to get foamy.

Add the melted butter and salt and whisk just until combined. Add the cocoa powder and 1 cup (135 g) of the flour and whisk on slow speed until combined. Then, add 2¼ cups (304 g) more of the flour and replace the whisk attachment with a dough hook. Start to knead the dough slowly and increase the speed to medium and then to high. Knead the dough for 5 to 10 minutes on high speed. The dough should be slightly sticky to the touch but should start to come off the sides of the bowl after a few minutes of kneading. If it continues to stick to the sides of the bowl after a few minutes of kneading, add 1 tablespoon (8 g) of flour at a time (up to ¼ cup [34 g] in total) and mix on low speed until the dough is of the right consistency; then, turn the speed back to high. Do not add more than ¼ cup (34 g) of flour, or your pretzel knots will be dry. In the end, the dough should be smooth, soft and lightly sticky, and the bowl should be clean without any dough on the sides.

Lightly spray a large, heatproof bowl with nonstick spray and transfer the dough to the bowl; lightly oil the top of the dough as well. Then, turn off the preheated oven and place the bowl, uncovered, in the oven, leaving the door ajar, for 30 to 45 minutes, or until doubled in size. Remove the bowl from the oven and preheat to 425°F (220°C).

(Continued)

Cinnamon Sugar Dark Chocolate Pretzel Knots with Chocolate Dipping Sauce (Continued)

½ cup (100 g) sugar

1½ tsp (4 g) ground cinnamon

¼ cup (57 g [½ stick]) unsalted butter, melted

CHOCOLATE DIP

3 oz (85 g) bar-style semisweet chocolate, finely chopped

½ cup (120 ml) heavy whipping cream

On a lightly floured surface, knead the dough a few times until all the air is released. Then, divide the dough into 10 equal-sized pieces. Roll one portion into a 6- to 7-inch (15- to 18-cm)-long rope and flatten with your fingers. Place one-tenth of the chopped chocolate in the center of the dough and pinch the side edges with your fingers to enclose the chocolate in the center of the dough. Roll the dough with your fingers into a 20-inch (51-cm)-long rope. Fold the rope in half around your finger and twist a couple of times, then tuck the ends of the rope through the hole where your finger was. Repeat until all 10 pretzel knots are prepared, then set aside.

In a large saucepan over high heat, bring the 10 cups (2.4 L) of water and all the baking soda to a rolling boil. Using a large, flat, slotted spatula, place one pretzel at a time in the boiling water and boil for 20 to 30 seconds. Remove the pretzels as soon as they have been cooked and arrange 5 pretzels, 2 to 3 inches (5 to 7.5 cm) apart on each prepared baking sheet. Brush the tops of the pretzel knots lightly with the beaten egg. Bake one baking sheet at a time for 12 to 14 minutes, or until they are dark golden brown.

Remove from the oven and let cool on the pan for 5 to 10 minutes, or until they are cool enough to touch.

Meanwhile, make the cinnamon sugar coating: In a small bowl, combine the sugar and cinnamon. Lightly brush each warm pretzel knot with melted butter and then roll in or sprinkle with the cinnamon sugar. Let cool for 30 minutes.

Make the chocolate dip: Place the chocolate in a heatproof bowl and set aside. In a microwave-safe bowl, microwave the cream on a medium setting until it starts to simmer, 1 to 2 minutes. Pour over the chocolate and let sit for 2 minutes, then stir until smooth and combined. Let cool for 10 minutes before serving.

To eat, dunk the fresh pretzel knots in the chocolate dip. The pretzel knots are best eaten fresh and on the same day. However, you can store leftovers in an airtight container at room temperature for up to 1 day.

NOTE: If you skip the cinnamon sugar coating, you can extend the storage life of the knots for 1 more day. It's delicious either way. Reheat the dip in the microwave if it gets too firm.

The day has come. The day on which you learn how to make irresistible, superflaky—and I mean super, superflaky—homemade chocolate croissants. It's a special and rewarding feeling to watch your family's eyes start glowing as they tear into the croissants you spent so much time on. That electrifying moment makes all the hard work worth it, I promise! Oh, and before you even jump into the recipe, I would like to point out that even though I provided the measuring in cups, I highly recommend using grams for every ingredient when making croissants, to get the best possible results.

Ultraflaky Chocolate Croissants (Pain au Chocolat)

YIELD: 14 CROISSANTS

3⅔ cups plus ½ tbsp (500 g) all-purpose flour, plus more for dusting

¼ cup (50 g) sugar

3¼ tsp (10 g) active dry yeast

6½ tsp (90 g) cold milk

½ cup (113 g [1 stick]) unsalted butter, at room temperature

2 tsp (12 g) salt

½ cup (120 g) cold water

1¼ cups (283 g [2½ sticks]) cold unsalted butter

4.5 oz (128 g) bar-style semisweet chocolate, chopped into long, thin pieces

1 large egg

1 large egg yolk

3 to 4 cups (720 to 960 ml) boiling water

In a large bowl, using an electric mixer fitted with a dough hook, mix the flour, sugar, yeast, milk, ½ cup (113 g) of room-temperature butter and salt on low speed until the dough starts to come together. With the mixer running, slowly add the cold water until completely incorporated. Then, increase the speed to medium-low and knead the dough for 10 minutes.

Remove the dough from the bowl and use your hands to shape it into a 10 x 6¾-inch (25 x 17–cm) rectangle. Wrap the dough tightly with plastic wrap and refrigerate overnight for about 12 hours.

Prepare the remaining butter on the same day as the dough: Place the cold butter between 2 pieces of parchment or waxed paper and pound it with a rolling pin into a 7 x 7-inch (18 x 18-cm) rectangle. Using the palm of your hands, straighten the outer edges by pushing the sides toward the center. Roll the butter until evenly thick. Wrap tightly in plastic wrap and refrigerate overnight along with the croissant dough.

Remove the dough from the fridge and place it in the freezer for 20 minutes. The butter and the dough should be almost the same firmness.

On a very lightly floured surface, roll the dough into a 15 x 8-inch (38 x 20-cm) rectangle. Place the butter slab on one-half of the croissant dough so that there is about a ½-inch (1.3-cm) space around the three outer edges and fold the other half of the dough over the butter. Completely seal the edges of the dough by pressing them together with your fingers. Make sure that there are no air bubbles between the layers and that the butter is completely covered. Rotate the dough by 90 degrees.

(Continued)

Ultraflaky Chocolate Croissants (Pain au Chocolat) (Continued)

Using as little flour as necessary for the dough not to stick, firmly but carefully press the dough with the rolling pin, starting at both sealed ends (see photo 1). Then, stop pressing and begin to roll the croissant dough, always being careful not to overwork it; otherwise, the butter will incorporate with the dough. Roll the dough just in one direction backward and forward into a 15 x 8-inch (38 x 20-cm) rectangle, making sure that you lengthen the dough instead of widening it and keep the edges as straight as possible. Rotate the dough by 180 degrees and also flip it upside down while rolling to keep it even, if needed. Shape the corners with your hands so that the dough is a true rectangle and not an oval (see photo 2).

Remove all excess flour from the dough before folding it, if there is some. Being careful to fold the croissant dough slowly enough that it doesn't rip or break, take one short side and fold one-third of the dough over itself, so about two-thirds of the dough is covered by itself. Then, take the other short side and flip it over itself so that it touches the edge of the previously folded part. The croissant dough is now one-third of its original size (see photo 3). Then, fold it in half. You should now have a rectangle with four layers of dough (see photo 4). Be sure that you remove all excess flour between each layer. Cover the dough tightly with plastic wrap and freeze for 30 minutes.

Roll the dough in the direction of the two open ends, with the fold to your right, until it is again a 15 x 8-inch (38 x 20-cm) rectangle. Using only as little flour as possible, and working slowly and remembering to keep the edges straight, rotate the dough by 180 degrees and flip while you roll it to keep it even, if necessary. As in the previous step, lift a short side of the croissant dough and fold one-third of the dough over itself to create a section 2 layers thick. Then, take the other short end and fold it on top so that it covers the first short end, like a folded business letter, to make three layers. Wrap the dough again in plastic wrap and chill in the refrigerator overnight, about 12 hours.

Rotate the dough again by 90 degrees from the previous position and roll it into a 26 x 10½-inch (66 x 27-cm) rectangle about ⅛ inch (4 mm) thick. And again, using as little flour as possible, keeping the edges as straight as possible and not overworking the dough, use your hands to gently square the corners of the dough.

Using a very sharp knife or pizza cutter, cut off a scant ½ inch (1 cm) from every edge to reveal the multilayered puff pastry on all sides. The dough should be about 25 x 9½ inches (64 x 25 cm) now. Use a tape measure or yardstick to measure both short sides of the dough and mark the center of each short side. Then, cut the dough in half, connecting the 2 marks, to create 2 long rectangles roughly 25 x 4¾ inches (64 x 12.5 cm). Now, using the same measuring and cutting tools as earlier, measure both long sides and divide their length by seven. Cut each dough portion into seven equal-sized rectangles; each should be roughly 3½ x 4¾ inches (9 x 12.5 cm). Place the chopped chocolate on a short side of each dough portion and roll up the dough tightly.

Line three baking sheets with parchment paper and place 4 or 5 croissants on each baking sheet, leaving enough space between the croissants so they have room to rise. Depending on how active the yeast is, the croissants will triple in size (ideally). Place the ends of the croissants underneath themselves that they don't unroll during baking.

(Continued)

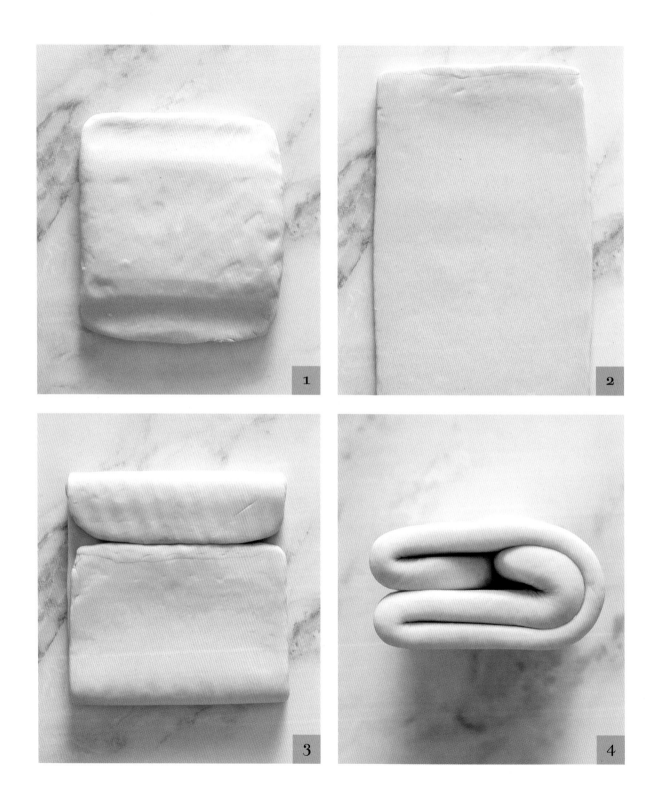

Ultraflaky Chocolate Croissants (Pain au Chocolat) (Continued)

In a small cup, combine the egg and egg yolk and lightly brush the croissants with the mixture, reserving what has not been used. Then, place a pan of boiling hot water on the bottom of your oven and arrange the two baking sheets with the croissants on the racks above. Close the oven door and let the croissants proof for 2½ hours. By that time, they should be tripled in size and slightly wobbly when you shake the baking sheet.

Remove all the pans, including the water pan, from the oven and preheat to 375°F (190°C). Carefully brush the croissants a second time with the egg mixture. Bake one sheet at a time for 16 to 20 minutes, or until evenly browned.

Remove from the oven and let cool on the baking sheet for 5 minutes, then transfer to a wire rack to cool completely.

Chocolate croissants are best eaten fresh on the same day. However, you can store them in an airtight container at room temperature up to 2 days.

NOTE: The boiling hot water in the oven simulates a professional oven and keeps your croissants from drying out. However, please watch the temperature in the oven and your croissants during the proofing time, especially in the beginning, so that it doesn't get warmer than 78°F (26°C). If it gets any warmer than that, leave the oven door ajar. Otherwise, the butter may start to melt.

This is perfect for breakfast because it fills you up with all the chocolate love you need to head into a great day. If you feel that your brioche is getting dry after storing it, just place a slice in a microwave for 20 to 30 seconds before eating; it will get soft again. And imagine a warm slice of brioche bread with, let's say, chocolate spread on top. Just fabulous, darling.

Double Chocolate Raisin Brioche Bread

YIELD: **12** SERVINGS

½ cup (120 ml) lukewarm milk (110°F [43°C])

⅜ cup (75 g) sugar

2¼ tsp (7 g) active dry yeast

2 large eggs

½ cup (113 g [1 stick]) unsalted butter, melted

1 tsp vanilla extract

½ tsp salt

¼ cup (21 g) unsweetened Dutch-processed cocoa powder, spooned and leveled

2½ to 2¾ cups (338 to 371 g) all-purpose flour, spooned and leveled

½ cup (80 g) raisins

½ cup (85 g) semisweet chocolate chips

Nonstick spray, for bowl

1 large egg, lightly beaten

Preheat the oven to 200°F (100°C).

In a large bowl, using an electric mixer fitted with a whisk attachment, stir together the milk, sugar and yeast. Then, let the mixture sit for 5 to 10 minutes, or until the surface starts to get foamy.

Add the eggs, melted butter, vanilla and salt and whisk just until combined. Add the cocoa powder and 1 cup (135 g) of the flour and whisk on slow speed until combined. Then, add 1½ cups (203 g) of the flour and the raisins and chocolate chips and replace the whisk attachment with a dough hook. Start to knead the dough slowly and increase the speed to medium and then to high. Knead for 5 to 10 minutes on high speed. The dough should be slightly sticky to the touch but should start to come away from the sides of the bowl after a few minutes of kneading. If it continues to stick to the sides of the bowl after a few minutes of kneading, add 1 tablespoon (8 g) of flour at a time (up to ¼ cup [34 g] in total) and mix on low speed until the dough is of the right consistency; then, turn the speed back to high. Do not add more than ¼ cup (34 g) of flour, or your brioche bread will be dry. In the end, the dough should be smooth, soft and lightly sticky, and the bowl should be clean without any dough on the sides.

Lightly spray a large, heatproof bowl with nonstick spray and transfer the dough to the bowl; lightly oil the top of the dough as well. Then, turn off the preheated oven and place the bowl, uncovered, in the oven for 15 minutes, leaving the oven door ajar.

Remove the bowl from the oven and preheat to 200°F (100°C) again. Line a baking sheet with parchment paper and set aside.

(Continued)

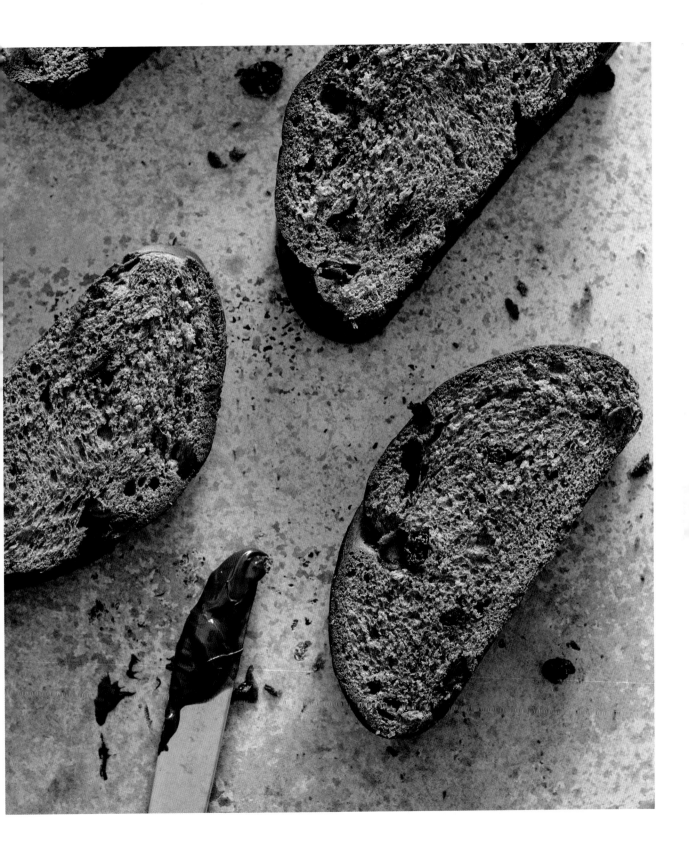

Double Chocolate Raisin Brioche Bread (Continued)

On a lightly floured surface, knead the dough a few times until all the air is released. Then, divide the dough into three equal-sized portions and roll them into three 20-inch (51-cm)-long logs. Place all three logs next to each other and pinch together the upper end of the strands. Then, braid the strands by alternately folding the right strand over the middle strand and placing it into the middle, then folding the left strand over the middle strand and placing it into the middle. Once the braid is completed, tuck both tips of the brioche bread under so it has a round shape and pinch the ends so they hold together.

Transfer the bread to the baking sheet and place in the oven. Turn off the oven and, leaving the oven door ajar, let the bread rise for 30 minutes. Then, remove the baking sheet from the oven and preheat to 375°F (190°C).

Lightly brush the bread with the beaten egg and bake for 28 to 30 minutes, covering the bread loosely with parchment paper or foil after 10 minutes to prevent it from heavily browning, if necessary.

Remove the bread from the oven and let cool on the baking sheet for about 1 hour.

Although brioche bread is best eaten fresh, you can store it in an airtight container at room temperature up to 2 days.

NOTE: You can skip the raisins and replace them with additional chocolate chips, if preferred.

Expect a firework of flavors in your mouth when biting into these Danishes. The chocolate cream cheese and the homemade strawberry-chamomile jam are just dreamy with the fluffy chocolate brioche. All the flavors play so harmoniously together, it's as if they were meant for one another. If you don't like chamomile, you could skip adding the tea bags in the jam recipe. The chamomile flavor is just mild and not the star of this recipe, though. The chocolate is the star, as always.

Chocolate Cream Cheese Brioche Danishes with Strawberry-Chamomile Jam

YIELD: 12 BRIOCHE DANISHES

JAM

½ cup (120 ml) water

3 chamomile tea bags

1 tbsp (8 g) cornstarch

1 heaping cup (150 g) strawberries, hulled and pureed

½ cup (100 g) sugar

1 tbsp (15 ml) fresh lemon juice

Pinch of salt

1 tsp vanilla extract

CREAM CHEESE FILLING

8 oz (227 g) cream cheese, softened

½ cup (100 g) sugar

2 tbsp (11 g) unsweetened natural cocoa powder

1 tsp vanilla extract

Make the jam: In a small saucepan, bring the water to a boil. Then, pour the water in a heatproof cup and add the tea bags. Let steep for 10 minutes, then discard the tea bags, add the cornstarch and stir to combine.

In a medium saucepan over medium-high heat, combine the strawberry puree, sugar, lemon juice, salt and the tea mixture and bring to a simmer. Cook for 5 to 10 minutes, or until thickened and reduced by half. Remove from the heat and stir in the vanilla. Cover and set aside.

Make the cream cheese filling: In a medium bowl, combine all the filling ingredients and whisk until smooth and no lumps remain. Refrigerate until you are ready to use.

(Continued)

Chocolate Cream Cheese Brioche Danishes with Strawberry-Chamomile Jam (Continued)

DOUGH

¾ cup (180 ml) lukewarm milk (110°F [43°C])

¼ cup (50 g) sugar

1 tbsp (9 g) active dry yeast

2½ cups (338 g) all-purpose flour, spooned and leveled, plus more for dusting

2 tbsp (11 g) unsweetened natural cocoa powder

¼ cup (57 g [½ stick]) cold unsalted butter

1 large egg, lightly beaten

1 tsp salt

1 large egg white

SERVING SUGGESTIONS

Fresh chamomile blossoms and chocolate sauce

Make the dough: In a large bowl, whisk together the milk, sugar and yeast. Then, cover the bowl tightly with plastic wrap and let sit at room temperature for 15 minutes.

Meanwhile, in a food processor, combine the flour, cocoa powder and butter and pulse just three or four times so that large butter flakes are still visible. Alternatively, cut the butter into ½-inch (1.3-cm) chunks, add to the flour mixture and stir to combine. Set aside.

Remove the plastic wrap from the yeast mixture, add the egg and salt to the bowl and whisk just until combined. Fold in the flour mixture just until the dough comes together; it won't be smooth at all. Cover the bowl tightly with plastic wrap and refrigerate overnight, 8 to 12 hours.

Transfer the dough to a lightly floured surface and roll it into a 15 x 15-inch (38 x 38-cm) rectangle. Then, fold the dough in thirds like a business letter and rotate by 90 degrees. Roll out, fold and turn two more times. Then, wrap the folded dough tightly in plastic wrap and refrigerate for 1 hour.

Preheat the oven to 400°F (205°C). Line two or three baking sheets with parchment paper and set aside.

Roll the folded dough into a ¼-inch (6-mm)-thick square and cut into 12 squares. For the shape you see in the picture, fold each square into triangles diagonally and turn so that the long side is toward you. Then, from each short side, cut about ¼ inch (6 mm) along the outside edge but not all the way up to the top point, so that the "frame" you have created is not cut completely through. Then, unfold the dough and fold the outer frame, which is pointing toward you over the square, until it touches the cut you made on the top. Then, fold the cut frame from the top and fold toward you that it touches the cut side facing you.

Place 1 tablespoon (15 ml) of the cream cheese filling and 1 to 2 tablespoons (15 to 30 ml) of the jam in the center of each brioche Danish. You may not need all of the jam. Arrange about 4 Danishes, spaced 3 inches (7.5 cm) apart, on each prepared baking sheet. Brush the edges of the dough with the egg white. Bake one sheet at a time for 8 to 10 minutes, or until the Danishes are puffy.

Remove from the oven and let cool for 30 minutes.

Serve immediately with the remaining jam and fresh chamomile blossoms, or chocolate sauce, if desired. Brioche Danishes are best eaten fresh and warm on the same day, but you can store leftovers in an airtight container for up to 1 day.

With this recipe, you can expect to have out-of-this-world flaky chocolate shortcakes filled with chocolate whipped cream, and served with a finger-licking pineapple rosemary sauce. It's just so good. We all know that shortcakes go well with strawberries, but give this sauce a try. It's very much worth it to explore new things when they're this tasty.

Pineapple Rosemary Dark Chocolate Shortcakes

YIELD: 12 SHORTCAKES

SAUCE

½ fresh pineapple, chopped into ½" (1.2-cm) pieces

¾ cup (150 g) sugar

½ cup (120 ml) water

1 tbsp (15 ml) fresh lemon juice

2 sprigs fresh rosemary

SHORTCAKES

2½ cups (338 g) all-purpose flour, spooned and leveled, plus more for dusting

¼ cup (21 g) unsweetened Dutch-processed cocoa powder, spooned and leveled

5 tsp (20 g) baking powder

¼ cup (50 g) sugar

½ tsp salt

½ cup (113 g [1 stick]) cold unsalted butter

1¼ cups (300 ml) buttermilk, divided

WHIPPED CREAM

1 cup (240 ml) heavy whipping cream

1 tbsp (8 g) powdered sugar

1½ tsp (3 g) unsweetened Dutch-processed cocoa powder

Make the sauce: In a small saucepan over medium heat, combine all the sauce ingredients and bring to a boil. Cook until thickened to the consistency of syrup, 5 to 10 minutes. Remove and discard the rosemary sprigs and set the sauce aside.

Make the shortcakes: Preheat the oven to 425°F (220°C). In a food processor, combine the flour, cocoa powder, baking powder, granulated sugar and salt in a food processor and pulse 2 to 3 times, or until evenly combined. Add the butter and pulse 4 or 5 times until pea-sized butter flakes are still visible.

Transfer the dough crumbs to a large bowl and make a well in the center. Add 1 cup (240 ml) of the buttermilk and fold until the dough comes together. The dough won't be smooth at all; do not overwork. On a lightly floured surface, shape the dough into a 9 x 13–inch (23 x 33-cm) rectangle. Then, fold the dough in thirds like a business letter and rotate by 90 degrees. Using just your fingers, flatten the dough again into a 9 x 13–inch (23 x 33–cm) rectangle and fold it again into thirds. Rotate by 90 degrees and then flatten and fold 1 more time.

Flatten the dough into a 10 x 13–inch (25 x 33–cm) rectangle and cut out twelve 3-inch (7.5-cm) circles. It's important that you press the cutter in a single strong downward motion without twisting the cutter. Otherwise, you will seal the edges of the shortcakes, and they won't rise. In a large cast-iron skillet or on a parchment paper–lined baking sheet, place the shortcakes very close to one another, touching. Then, brush them with the remaining buttermilk (you may not need all of it). Bake for 15 minutes. Remove from the oven and transfer to a wire rack to let the shortcakes cool for 30 minutes.

Make the whipped cream: In a large bowl, using an electric mixer fitted with a whisk attachment, whip the cream on medium speed for 2 to 3 minutes, or until soft peaks form. Then, add the powdered sugar and cocoa powder and whip until stiff peaks form, 1 to 2 minutes.

Cut the shortcakes in half horizontally and fill with the sauce and whipped cream. The shortcakes are best eaten fresh. You can store all three components separately for 2 days. I recommend storing the sauce and the cream in the fridge and the shortcakes at room temperature.

You are seriously going to lose your mind over these cream puffs. This recipe is exciting in so many ways: First, you'll learn how to make French pastry, called pâte à choux, which will open the world to all kinds of cream puffs, profiteroles, éclairs and croquembouches. Second, the white chocolate pastry cream is to die for. Third, the matcha glaze is just delicious. The matcha is very present but not overpowering. For the success of this recipe, the most crucial part is that you don't open the oven during the baking time. So, steady your nerves and keep the cream puffs in the oven for as long as the recipe states—without opening the door.

White Chocolate–Matcha Cream Puffs

YIELD: **26** TO **28** CREAM PUFFS

FILLING

3 large egg yolks

⅓ cup (67 g) sugar

¼ cup (32 g) cornstarch

1¼ cups (300 ml) milk

¾ cup (180 ml) heavy whipping cream

6 oz (170 g) bar-style white chocolate, finely chopped

2 tsp (10 ml) vanilla extract

⅛ tsp salt

PÂTE À CHOUX

1 cup (240 ml) water

½ cup (113 g [1 stick]) unsalted butter

1 tsp sugar

½ tsp salt

1 cup (135 g) all-purpose flour, spooned and leveled

4 large eggs

EGG WASH

1 large egg

1 tbsp (15 ml) water

Make the filling: In a medium bowl, whisk together the egg yolks, sugar and cornstarch to combine and set aside.

In a heavy-bottomed saucepan over medium-high heat, bring the milk and cream to a simmer and cook for 2 minutes, stirring constantly. Decrease the heat to low and whisk about ½ cup (120 ml) of the hot milk into the egg yolk mixture to slowly temper it. Then, slowly whisk the tempered egg yolk mixture into the saucepan and cook, whisking constantly, until the filling is thick, about 2 minutes.

Remove from the heat and stir in the chocolate, vanilla and salt until smooth and fully incorporated, 1 to 2 minutes. Pour the filling through a mesh strainer into a medium bowl and cover the surface with plastic wrap to prevent it forming a skin. Refrigerate the filling for at least 2 hours or overnight.

Make the pâte à choux: Preheat the oven to 375°F (190°C). Line two baking sheets with parchment paper and set aside.

Prepare the egg wash by combining the egg and water in a small bowl and set aside. In a heavy-bottomed saucepan over medium heat, bring the water, butter, granulated sugar and salt to a boil. Use a wooden spoon to stir in the flour constantly as you cook the dough for 2 to 3 minutes, or until it starts to form a film on the bottom of the pan.

Transfer the dough to a large bowl and let cool for about 2 minutes. Still using the wooden spoon, stir in one egg at a time. You will notice that after every addition, the dough will separate. Keep stirring until the dough comes together again before you add the next egg. Repeat until all the eggs are incorporated. In the end, the dough will be sticky and firm enough to hold a stiff peak.

(Continued)

White Chocolate–Matcha Cream Puffs (Continued)

2 cups (240 g) unpacked powdered sugar, sifted

1 tsp matcha powder

1 tsp vanilla extract

3 tbsp (45 ml) hot water

Transfer the dough to a piping bag and, spinning the piping tip as you go, pipe 1½-inch (4-cm) circles onto the prepared baking sheets. If the paper is shifting, you can stick a bit of dough to the baking sheets underneath the parchment paper so that the paper doesn't move as you pipe. Press down the tips of the dough with wet fingers to even them; otherwise, the tips may burn. Lightly brush the pâte à choux with egg wash. Bake one baking sheet at a time for 30 to 32 minutes, or until the pâte à choux is puffed and golden brown. Do not open the oven while baking, or the cream puffs will collapse.

Remove from the oven and let cool on the pans to room temperature, about 1 hour.

Make the glaze: In a large bowl, whisk together the powdered sugar, matcha powder and vanilla to combine. Add 1 tablespoon (15 ml) of hot water at a time and whisk to combine. Stop adding water when the consistency is thick but liquid. If the glaze is too thick, there will be too much glaze on the cream puffs. On the other hand, if it is too thin, it will run down the cream puffs. Test the consistency down the sides of your bowl for clarity.

Transfer the filling to a piping bag fitted with a round tip. Using the tip of a sharp knife, cut a little *X* into the bottom of each cream puff, then pipe the filling into the puffs. Dip the tops of the filled cream puffs into the glaze and place them on a wire rack to let dry.

Store leftover cream puffs in an airtight container in the refrigerator for up to 3 days.

NOTE: The single teaspoon of matcha powder seems little, but the taste is very intense and adding more matcha would overpower the taste of the cream puffs. That said, you can adjust the amount of matcha powder to your taste.

Acknowledgments

I would like to thank Jenna Fagan for going along with me in creating this cookbook. Thank you for your guidance throughout its creation. With you, this became the best chocolate cookbook it can be. I'm also thankful that you immediately fell in love with the idea of making a chocolate dessert book together. It was a wonderful and beautiful journey.

Special thanks to everyone at Page Street Publishing for making this book happen. With your help and professionalism, it became the book I've always dreamed of. This book is very tasteful and I just love every single detail about it. Thank you for guiding me through the photography process to make it not just a book with amazing recipes but also one with mouthwatering food photos.

A huge thank you to my dear husband, Mario. Without you, I wouldn't be where I am today and this book would never ever exist. You helped me in every stage of the process physically, and more important, mentally. To work on this cookbook alongside my business in as little as five months, while also moving house midway through, was a huge undertaking for me and us. You always supported me and had a huge influence on this cookbook. Without you, it would not be the book it is today. You are my best friend, lover, husband and soulmate. I love you!

To my mom, you always believed in me, and your never-ending support means so much to me and made me as strong as I am. I know that I can always count on you whatever happens in my life, and this makes you the best mother I could ask for. Thank you; I love you!

Last, but not least, a big, big thank-you to all of my readers. I made this chocolate cookbook for you. I hope you enjoy it and it will become one of your favorite cookbooks.

About the Author

SABINE VENIER is a recipe developer, photographer, videographer, food stylist and the founder of Also The Crumbs Please, where she regularly publishes easy-to-follow step-by-step baking recipes. Her recipes are published by magazines such as *Where Women Create* and also mentioned on websites such as Rachael Ray Everyday and Bake from Scratch. She won the PDN Taste Photography Award in 2018, and her stunning Galaxy Cake recipe video from her blog was a part of a commercial campaign for an internet provider in Canada. Find Sabine's recipes on her blog alsothecrumbsplease.com and her beautiful photography and videography work at sabinevenier.com.

Index